Soul Searchn'

AN EMOTIONAL LIFE JOURNEY OF POEMS

AND SHORT STORIES

DANA TOLIVER

ISBN 978-1-63784-515-8 (paperback)
ISBN 978-1-63784-516-5 (digital)

Copyright © 2024 by Dana Toliver

All rights reserved. No part of this publication may be reproduced, distributed, or transmitted in any form or by any means, including photocopying, recording, or other electronic or mechanical methods without the prior written permission of the publisher. For permission requests, solicit the publisher via the address below.

Hawes & Jenkins Publishing
16427 N Scottsdale Road Suite 410
Scottsdale, AZ 85254
www.hawesjenkins.com

Printed in the United States of America

DEDICATION

This book is dedicated, with love, to my daughter, **Jayla Hardrict**; and to Mariah Carey for writing and recording such a powerful song, *HERO*, which helped save my life!

In Loving Memory of Jazz Amira Hardrict
December 29, 2008 – September 5, 2022

CONTENTS

Introduction..xi

SECTION ONE: LOVE

1: My Little Angel 3
2: With Every Beat Of My Heart 4
3: In A Child's Eyes 5
4: Protect The Little Ones 6
5: Little Bird...7
6: Children...8
7: My Gift..9
8: Mother...10
9: Love Letter...11
10: Strong Enough 12
11: What Love 13
12: Reaching Out 15
13: Don't Understand...17
14: Unconditional Love..18
15: Am I Not Deserving.......................................20
16: No More Tears (A Mother's Love) 21
17: Sometimes..22
18: Acceptance...23
19: Memories...24
20: Just Because I Said Goodbye 25
21: Broken Down...27
22: So Long..28
23: He Doesn't Care 30
24: Fly Free 31

25:	All In Vain	32
26:	Heartache	33
27:	Lost In Translation	34
28:	You Will Never Find	35
29:	The One Who Loves You	36
30:	Love	37
31:	In Love	38
32:	Him	39
33:	Cloud Nine	40
34:	I Love Him	42
35:	Sad, Sad Situation	43
36:	Left With Nothing	45
37:	Because I Fell In Love	47
38:	Another Love Lost	48
39:	Tortured Soul	50
40:	Someone To Love	51
41:	Let It Rain	53
42:	Broken Man	55
43:	Your Love	56
44:	Torn	57
45:	Trauma	58
46:	Relationships	59
47:	Love Verses Hate	60
48:	The ABC's Of Love Is	61
49:	Night Might As Well Be Day	63
50:	Speak To Me Darling	64
51:	Queen	65
52:	Love And Fear	67
53:	Beauty Of The Sun	68
54:	Fear Not, Love All	69

SECTION TWO: MASK

55:	Mask	73
56:	C.R.A.Z.Y. (I Am Who I Am)	75
57:	Ever-Changing Winds	76

58:	Look To The Core	77
59:	Ambiguous	78
60:	Too Blind To See	79
61:	Born Like Me	80
62:	Nowhere	81
63:	Through The Storm	82
64:	Family Secrets	83
65:	Rose Petals	84
66:	One Kind Of Mother	85
67:	My Father's Son	87
68:	One Kind Of Father	88
69:	A Promise Made	89
70:	Should'a, Would'a, Could'a	90
71:	Just A Dream	91
72:	Sad To Know	92
73:	Dear Family	93
74:	Wrapped Up	94
75:	Closed In	95
76:	Private Hell	97
77:	Seed	98
78:	In My Eyes	99
79:	To Be Gone	100
80:	The Other Side	102
81:	Not Of This World	103
82:	What Will It Take	104
83:	Superwoman	105
84:	Rose Tinted Eyes	106
85:	Angel Of Me	108
86:	Reflection	109
87:	Gemini	110
88:	Unknown	111
89:	Simply Complex	112
90:	D.A.D.	113
91:	The Definition Of D.A.D.	114
92:	Lightbulb Moment	115
93:	Who Am I?	117

94: So True	118
95: My Life Story	120
96: My Life Story Continued	121
97: Handwriting Analysis	123
98: My Filing Cabinet Brain Memory Recall Analogy	125
99: Everything Changes (Clean Version)	126
100: In The Mirror	127
101: Mycotoxicosis	128
102: Journeys	131
103: Pseudo Mutuality	132

SECTION THREE: INSIGHT

104: I Have Found My Light	139
105: I Am Human	140
106: Words Of Wisdom	142
107: The Light	143
108: Spirit Soul	144
109: Wisdom	145
110: Spirituality Verses Religion	146
111: Ball And Chain	148
112: Insight	149
113: Choices	151
114: Quotes	152
115: Warning: Wake Up!	154
116: Freedom	156
117: Emotions	157
118: Do It Yourself	158
119: Con	159
120: Justification	160
121: Abuse	161
122: Rights	162
123: Reality	163
124: Being A Shorty	164
125: When Morning Comes	168
126: Peace	169

127: Leap Of Faith 170
128: Duality 171
129: Karma 173
130: Conventional Wisdom 174
131: Death, Fear, Destiny, Love, Karma 175
132: Ignorance Is Bliss 176
133: Faith 177
134: Mother Earth 178
135: Quotes Two 180
136: State Of Living 181
137: And The Journey Continues 184

SECTION FOUR: INSANITY

138: What's This World Coming To? 187
139: Quotes Three 188
140: Lost In The Streets 190
141: Come To Peace 191
142: Quotes Four 192
143: The World Today 193
144: Forgive Us 194
145: Quotes Five 195
146: The Question 197
147: Credit Cards 198
148: Money ($) 199
149: Euro-Centricity 200
150: Quotes Six 201
151: High Class Pimps 203
152: Pyramid Scheme 204
153: Lies 205
154: Congress 206
155: Insanity 207
156: Quarter Analogy 208
157: Hollywood Car Analogy 209
158: Ten Percent 210
159: Quotes Seven 211

160: The Fungus Among Us 213
161: Face The Reality 215
162: Secret Illusion... 217
163: Quotes Eight.. 218
164: Collective Conscience 220
165: Guardian Angels.. 222
166: The Devil 224
167: Rainbow.. 225

SECTION FIVE: IN MEMORY

168: Granddaddy 229
169: Man (1998) 230
170: I Saw A Man 231
171: Nine.. 232
172: Through The Darkness (Ben)...................................... 233
173: A Moment In Time (Tim)... 234
174: Carrie.. 235
175: The Day The Sun Fell Down 236
176: A Star Is Born (jiji) 237
177: Misty Blue... 238
178: September Rain... 239
179: Jazz... 240
180: R.I.P. – The Day They Found PEACE 242

SECTION SIX: APPRECIATION

181: Acknowledgements.. 247
182: A Tribute To Mariah... 249

INTRODUCTION

This book is a collection of poems, short stories and quotes woven together to capture moments of my life's journey. It covers a range of topics and is unconventional, controversial, emotional yet inspirational and insightful.

    I never, consciously, set out to write a book; it started out as me journaling as therapy, *SOUL SEARCH'N*, which turned into writing my first poem back in 1990. From there, I kept writing over the years and realized the collection of poems and short stories I was accumulating told a story so I turned what I wrote into this book.

    I know that everyone has a story and is on their own journey of discovery, however, I also know that there are many people going through similar circumstances, trials and tribulations that I have been through. My hope is that with this book people will know that they are not alone.

Enjoy,
Dana Toliver

SECTION ONE

LOVE

My Little Angel

As the tears roll down my cheek
oh, how I cry for her
The sorrow it brings
to my heart and soul to see her weep

As she cries for him
tears fall upon my face
As I see her face swell from all the tears
I hold her in my arms
and gently rock her to sleep

Sweet dreams my little angel
Mommy loves you
I always will with all my heart and soul

As you try to be strong
I know that you are crying inside
I know your heart is breaking
and I know you feel as though you are all alone
but I am here to reassure you, you are never alone

You will never have to question my love for you
I will always be there for you
I'll always be around for you
If not face-to-face then always in your heart

Look to the sky and you will find
that sign coming down from the heavens above

I love you my little angel – stay sweet!

With Every Beat Of My Heart

With every beat of my heart, I shall
cherish your every breath

With every beat of my heart, I shall
love you unconditionally

With every beat of my heart, I shall
say a prayer on your behalf

With every beat of my heart, I shall
support the dreams that flow
through your heart

With every beat of my heart, I shall
remember you are your own spirit

With every beat of my heart, I shall
respect the spirit of who you are

With every beat of my heart, I shall
make this a promise!

In A Child's Eyes

You should see light
in a child's eyes
You should see innocence
in a child's eyes
You should see peace
in a child's eyes
And you should see joy
in a child's eyes

But if you do not
then you know
you are looking at
a child whose spirit
has been lost

Protect The Little Ones

We have to be their eyes
We have to be their ears
We have to be the ones to calm their fears

They don't know who to trust
so, you and I must see them through
these tender years

No matter what the race
a child is an innocent face

We must accept the blame
when they feel pain
We must protect our little ones
They are the future!

Little Bird

She's like a little bird
sitting in a nest
waiting for answers
from her mother

Her big brown eyes
gaze into the star-filled sky

My job is to clear the path
that will someday lead to her success
If she fails then I have failed

She's like a bird without wings
waiting to fly free!

Children

Children have their own
hearts, minds and souls

Allow them to choose
their own path

Do not choose their path for them

Allow them to follow their own
heart, their own mind
and their own spirit

Do not force your own desires
and beliefs onto them

Otherwise you stunt their growth
and they grow up to be resentful, bitter adults
for not giving them their wings to fly
and be free to touch the sky

My Gift

She gives me strength to carry on
She gives me courage to keep fighting
She gives me love that fills my heart
She truly is my gift from heaven above

Mother

I chose to become a mother
Now I have to live up to that title
and that is the hardest thing on this earth
I will ever have to do!

Love Letter

If for some reason
I do not make it through
My apologies
and know that I fought for you

Something went wrong
but our bond is strong
and even though I may be gone
My love for you always lives on

Scared to leave you all alone
and even though there are others
to lean on
There is no greater love
like a mother's love

I hope and pray to see another day
Afraid to close my eyes and sleep
I don't want to die and leave you behind
or have to say bye-bye

This is my love letter to you
from my heart
wish we never had to part

Always and forever
I love you

Strong Enough

I wish I could have been strong enough
to be a little more selfish
and not worried so much about my family

I just hope you are strong enough
to be a little more selfish than me
and live your life free

Don't worry about us
we'll be alright

The butterfly has a lot of meaning for me
but it also has a lot of meaning for you

That scorpio has to grow its wings
and fly farther than I

Don't let us bring you down
Be strong enough to fly high
Be strong enough to sail across the seas
to climb the highest mountains
and reach your every dream

I hope you will be strong enough
to be a little more selfish than me
and live your life forever free

What Love

We all just need
A little bit of understanding
Can not grasp
What you are not comprehending?
Knowing what I've known
Ever since I was four years old
Having to keep the secrets
Locked deep inside
I innately knew I would be
Travelin' a rough road, alone
Love? What love?
Never felt it
Through all the materialistic stuff
Being thrown at us
Can't face the truth
Of your own self-centeredness
And resentments you keep suppressed inside
Emotionless
Only giving to receive the praises
Of those outside looking in
Can we stop the madness?
Why would you sit by?
And watch me die?!
Don't understand the pain I feel?
Both physical and emotional
From the insensitivity
Won't accept me for me
Won't accept reality
Scared of vulnerability
When will you take responsibility?

Your anxiety breeds insecurity
Love? What love?
I wish I had the wings of a dove
So I could fly away
to the skies above and find real love!

Reaching Out

I am reaching out for your love
a mother's love, unconditional
but I am invisible
Can't see me as I am

How could she turn, walk away
and leave me so all alone
out there in the cold?

I am reaching out to you
my higher power in this darkest hour
Won't you please wash away
these tears I cry?
Take away my fears inside, I hide

I am reaching out for someone
to lend me a helping hand
Throw me a lifeline
before I drown in the despair
Won't somebody, please, care?

I am reaching out to a world divided
asking for your help to save us from ourselves

So sad to see so many
suffering needlessly

I am reaching out to emptiness
Reaching out to loneliness
Longing for some happiness

I am reaching out to you
my higher power in this darkest hour
Please, wash away my tears I cry
Please, take away these fears inside, I hide

Don't Understand

No one sees behind closed doors
the deafening silence, the isolation
the ice cold air and the neglect we all shared

The knives stabbing you in the back
chipping away, day after day
caused shattered dreams
and your heart to crumble

Left out in the cold all alone
to pick up the shattered pieces
of my broken heart, always living on the edge
with the weight of the world on my shoulders
on the verge of dying, I fell right over

Don't understand why in my times of desperation
they turn their faces away and act as though
they don't see the trials and tribulations

There is no escaping
the spiritless souls around me
bringing black clouds to cover me
keeping me sheltered from the truth
of this world that surrounds me

Don't understand why
they say they love me and tell me lies
I, just, don't understand why
they like to see me suffer and make me cry
time after time

Unconditional Love

Conditional love is all I know
It's not the typical love
or average dysfunction
It's dysfunction so deep
you are scarred for life

To be used by your family
to be labeled the black sheep
All it can do is make you weak

To realize as an adult
from the time you were conceived
you were never going to have
a chance to succeed
When your family sets it up
for you to fail

If you can't turn to your family
for unconditional love, support and guidance
then who can you turn to?

You try time and time again to reach out
to someone on the outside only to discover
conditional love that much worse

With no family and no friends
where is one to turn?

Just to know that somebody
somewhere out there truly cares
would be nice

All I am asking for is that
Unconditional love we all seek

Am I Not Deserving

Am I not deserving of respect
I know I have this affect on guys
who lose their minds
I catch their wandering eyes
as I walk by

Only wanted for my body
not for my heart or mind
Why are they so blind?
Can't see the good
deep down inside

I deserve a little bit of heaven
for all that I have given

So tired of being taken for granted
tired of being rejected, neglected and disrespected

Am I not worthy of a wedding ring
deserving of some wedding bliss
of a little bit of happiness

Though I have this affect
am I not deserving of respect?

No More Tears (A Mother's Love)

There's no more tears left to cry
I'm well aware of who she is
She left our hearts empty and dry
Been judged my whole life
For speaking out against the chaos and the confusion
But I've grown numb to the abuse and delusions
Never asked to be born into this
Or sent back here to the abyss
Where a mother's love doesn't exist

There's no more tears left to cry
I'm well aware of what she is, so cold inside
She left our hearts empty and dry
As she turned away and watched us fall
And pretended like she couldn't see
We tried to make it through the darkness
But couldn't see the light
Of where a mother's love ought to be

There's no more tears left to cry
As I come out of the darkness and say goodbye
To all the chaos and confusion
It's time to rise above it all and fly…

Sometimes

Sometimes I just need a hug
Sometimes I just need a shoulder to lean on
Sometimes I just need for someone to listen
Sometimes I just need to feel loved
Sometimes I just need a little understanding
Sometimes I just need to be acknowledged
Sometimes I just need a shoulder to cry on
Sometimes I just need to feel like I'm wanted
Sometimes I just need to hear your voice
Sometimes I just need someone there to catch me when
    I fall
and sometimes I just need you!

Acceptance

You have never accepted me
for who I truly am
so how will you ever be able
to accept her for who
she is and will become?

Someday, like me, she will become
a woman full of emotions

Memories

Memories of the way we used to be
Now that I am free my eyes can see

I tell myself I've got to be strong
but even though my fears are gone
I can't look to tomorrow
there is too much sorrow

I know holding on to your past
is nothing more than fearing the future

Although I'm ready to move on
from the memories of yesterday
I can still only live for today
I am not, yet, ready
for the new light of day

Memories of the way we used to be
Now that I am free my eyes can, finally, see

Just Because I Said Goodbye

Just because
I said goodbye
didn't mean
we had to cry
Our friendship
will always be but sometimes
friends must part so their spirits
can continue to grow

Like a caged animal
your spirit will die
if you hold on too tight or too long
If things said are truly meant
there won't be a sad song

Just because
I'm saying goodbye
doesn't mean you need
to be as cold as ice
It only tells me you are
blind a s mice

Actions speak
louder than words, you know
The light shines
straight through
that hole in your heart
Can't hide it anymore
I'm hip to your game
you should feel shame
you thought you were smart

Just because
I say goodbye
doesn't mean
we have to cry
be happy I have
let you go
now you can, finally
have the show

No more sharing
that's not so good
it means
no more caring
maybe we should?

Still be like the stem
and the bud of a flower
or maybe things
have gone too sour?

Just because
I said goodbye
didn't mean
we had to cry
I simply gave you
your space so don't let
the memories
in your mind
keep you haunted
It is exactly
what you wanted!

Broken Down

Broken down, knees on the ground
Longing for someone to love
To reach me and help me shine
And be forever mine

The times you feel so alone
Wishing for a warm embrace
but the broken in you makes you hesitate

The record might be skipping a beat
But I promise if you come vibe with me
We'll ride together on love's frequency

I'm still open to receiving the unconditional love
That I've longed for
and even though I'm battered and bruised
I'm still open to loving you and willing to try with you

So please send me a sign I can follow
To find love's divinity, I want serenity

I'm broken but still open to love
Because true love's a gift I am not willing to miss

So Long

Four months ago
you held him close
but now he's gone
it is such a shame
there is no one to blame
time makes it seem
like it is all a game

You are left alone
to ponder why
you can only assume
it is too late for your fate

Why can't he see
that it is meant to be?

Don't want to watch
him pass you by
How can somebody sit by
and see you cry
and not even bother
to ask you why
your head always wanders
so high in the clouds

Like a top
your mind is always spinning
only it knows when it will stop
Not knowing where you are

at times you get lost
lost in a world that feels
like a dream

You don't know where
to go from here but you know
you must be strong
or things will go wrong

As sad as it seems
you know you must find a way
to let go of all the pain, let it out
and then you can shout
I am free, free from all the misery

Four months ago
you held him close
but now he is gone
so you must find a way
to say so long

He Doesn't Care

It isn't fair that you don't care
about all the lies you share

It cuts like a knife
and rips me apart
All the deceit you keep

You look me in my eyes
and straight to my face
you boldly tell me lies

It's such a disgrace

I hope for your child's sake, someday
you change your manipulating ways

He doesn't care what he does to you
He doesn't care that he is hurting you

It breaks your heart
and rips you apart
all the deceit he keeps

It isn't fair that you don't care
About all the lies you share

Fly Free

You became my butterfly
I let you fly
but you did not return
to me

I guess we were never
meant to be
so I am letting you go

Fly free
as far as the wind will take you
as high as the clouds will carry you

Spread your wings
because I am ready
to spread my wings
and fly

as far as the wind will take me
as high as the clouds will carry me

It's time to say goodbye

All In Vain

I know, now, you like to see me suffer
I know, now, you like to cause me pain
I married you in vain!

Heartache

He doesn't know I cry at night
wishing he was here not there

My heart is breaking, truly aching
What's a girl like me to do?

I won't settle for second best
I won't settle for anything less
I only want what is best

He doesn't see things I see
He doesn't see reality
for we may never be

Facing your fears
makes you want to disappear

It's not just you
It's my family, too

My heart is aching, truly breaking
What's a girl like me to do?

I won't settle for second best
I won't settle for anything less
I only want what is best!

Lost In Translation

The misinterpretation of my words
Lost in translation
We have different definitions
Of friendship
Trying to avoid any
Heartbreak
All I needed was the truth
From the beginning
Spoken from the heart
Laid out on the table
And everything would have been
Alright
I didn't want to get burned
By the fire
But having a straight forward
Upfront conversation
Is like pulling teeth
There is no harm in going out
To have a sit down
Heart to heart
The only way to get to know someone
Is to spend time with them
There is no harm in going out
To have some fun as friends
If you truly are friends
Now all that is left
Is a mess of misunderstandings
And a wish to turn back
The hands of time

You Will Never Find

You will never find
someone more giving, more open
more caring and more loving than me

Yes, I have my flaws but don't we all?

Yes, it's true, baby, I want you

You will see no one will be
more honest and more loyal than me

The only way to understand me
is to step into my world and get to know me

So take a chance because I know
you will never find someone more giving
more open, more caring, more loving
more honest and more loyal than me

That I guarantee!

The One Who Loves You

The one who loves you
will bring you hope

The one who loves you
will give you strength

The one who loves you
will stick by your side
through thick and thin

The one who loves you
will always be there

The one who loves you
will stay

The one who loves you
won't go away

Love

Love is opening up your soul
like a flower blooming
you have to be vulnerable
and trust that things will be okay

If you can believe in your heart and mind
that things will be alright
you will make it through the night

Just like a flower blooming
after the rain falls
love grows

In Love

Love is not infatuation
it is not lust

Love means you know
how to let go

When you are willing
to set someone free
you give them their wings
to fly

If you are truly in love
you will know when
to say goodbye

Him

There is, just, something about him that I love
the way he looks, the way he laughs
the way he makes sweet love to me

I want to hold him in my arms
and never let go
watch the moon and stars through the night
until we see the morning light

Here in the dark
I hope and pray
that he will stay

If, only, dreams would come true
I wouldn't be sitting here so blue

There's, just, something about him
the way he looks, the way he laughs
the way he makes sweet love to me

There is, just, something about him that I love

Cloud Nine

You've got me feeling high
I feel so high I can almost touch the sky
I can not deny the way you make me feel inside

I, only, wish you were mine
then everything would be, just, fine
The flutters I feel deep down inside
the aching of my heart would all disappear

To know that I'd have you to come home to
to know I'd have you to hold me through the night
would make everything alright

I feel like I'm floating on cloud nine
when your body is next to mine
like a dove, there's peace I feel
whenever I'm by your side

We fit together like a hand in a glove
Could this be love?

Like a chocolate sundae with a cherry on top
You've got me feeling high, so high
I can almost touch the sky
I can't deny the way you make me feel inside

Like a kid in a candy store, I want more
you are the cherry in my life
What I would do, just, to be your wife!

You've got me feeling so high
I feel like I'm floating on cloud nine
I, only, wish you were mine
then everything would be, just, fine!

I Love Him

I will climb
to the highest mountain-top
fall on bended knees
raise my hands to the sky
and call his name

I have no shame
I love him

I will sail
across a thousand seas
I will fly
around the world
just to be by his side

There is no shame
in calling out his name

In my darkest hour
he's my light of day
I want the world to know
just how much I love him

I will climb
to the highest mountain-top
fall on bended knees
raise my hands to the sky
and call out his name

I have no shame
I love him!

Sad, Sad Situation

I have found the one guy for me
but it's a sad, sad, situation you see
because we can never ever be

Why would he go and lie to me
and tell me that he was free
when he knew all along
we were never meant to be

He played a sad, sad, song for me
he told me we would always be
but like a moth to a flame
I got burned by the fire

Blinded by the rays of the sun
I got lost in the haze
Blinded by his hypnotic gaze
I am trapped in the maze

I can't escape the heartache and pain
I gave all my love in vain

Why'd he go and lie to me
and tell me he as free
when he knew all along
we could never ever be

Together, as one
I've come undone
and now I've realized, over time
he will never be mine

I thought I found the one guy for me
but it's a sad, sad, situation you see
because we can never ever be

Left With Nothing

I left with nothing
but the clothes on my back
left everything behind
to escape the burning flames

I never thought
I had the strength
to leave

He tried to destroy my life
but I was stronger
than he ever thought

I was knocked down
over and over and over again
but rose out of the ashes

You tried to take my life
but I'm still here
still standing with no fear

It was the day he disrespected her
that I knew for sure
we were better off without him

Had I stayed
I know I would no be
writing this page

All the tears I've cried
and the lonely nights I spent
with no one by my side

Help him, please, to see
all the pain he's caused her and me

I won't keep running myself
into the same wall just to fall
over and over and over again

Left with nothing!

Because I Fell In Love

You stole my heart then walked away
and left me all alone

As I face another endless night
I never thought you'd misled me
but you played with my head
and my mind, you were so unkind

Why'd you play these games with me?
Baby, you've got the best of me
Why'd you go and set me free?
Can't you see you took my dreams
away from me?

Now I'm flying without wings
as I face the bitter cold
Please, don't let my dreams fade away
Baby, I just want you to stay
If, only, I could have one more chance with you
I would tell you I love you, today

No strings attached, no rings to hold you back
Do you really care for me? I need to know
Please, don't go

I just can't stand another minute away from you
because I fell in love with you

Another Love Lost

I once held you in my arms
but now you're gone
You say you want to see me happy
So come home where you belong

What happened to us?

Somehow along the way
the communication was lost
our signals were crossed

Another love lost

You say you still love me
you say you still care
so why won't you share

It's not about going back
but starting over
so why aren't you here?

Throw away your fear

I understand the reluctancy
but it's an atrocity to see
we may never be

Night after night
the emotions run deep, so I weep

I once held you in my arms
but now you're gone
come home where you belong

What happened to us?

Somehow along the way
the communication
was lost, our signals
were crossed

It's just another love lost

Tortured Soul

Tortured soul, the heart you stole
Broken down and devastated
after everything we've been
I have got to let you go, again
It hurts too much, now, to just be friends

I'm physically weak from this heartache
and emotionally and spiritually drained
but with so much love to give
The sorrow I hold is too heavy a load
I need the strength of a mustard seed
Just to hold on to my sanity

Like a moth to a flame, I see the fire
and have the desire to want to put out the fire
but every time I do I get burned by the bugs
that are attracted to my light

I'm so tired of the fight
and standing alone outside in the cold
Please, won't somebody let me in
so I can warm my tortured soul?

Someone To Love

I don't know what to do
I don't know what to think
I don't know how to feel
lost in a world, all alone
'cause no one's home

I just want someone to love me
someone to care
I just want someone to love
someone to care for me
don't you see
I need someone to love me for me

Nobody knows all of the pain
that I have inside
all the anguish that torments my mind
paranoia sets in

They don't understand
what goes through my mind
at times I want to breakdown and die
but instead I just cry
paralyzed from the heartache and pain
of not having someone to love

Can anybody out there hear me
or will I have to spend the rest of my life
with these chains locked around my heart?
I feel all torn apart

Lord, I need you, now
'cause I don't know
what to do, what to think or how to feel

I'm just lost in a world
so all alone
and no one's home

I just want someone
to love me
someone to care
I just want someone
to love
someone to care for me
don't you see
I need someone to
love me for me

Let It Rain

Let it rain
Let it pour
Let it thunder
Let it storm

To was away the heartache
and the pain of this game
I don't want to play
not even for one more day

Let it rain
Let it pour
Let it thunder
Let it storm

To wash away the sins of this world
so the lighting can be
turned into the light that brightens
the night to our path of right

For forty days and forty nights
until my heart can mend
when this cold cruel world sees an end
to all its sins and the new world begins

Until he knows all the love I have for him
and it resonates through every ounce of his soul
Show him, teach him, just how much I love him

I want to scream and shout out

Let it rain
Let it pour
Let it thunder
Let it storm

Broken Man

To the broken man I love
I see the strength and the fight within
you've got the strength to win
you will rise again from the ashes
like a Phoenix you will soar higher than ever before

To all those that doubted
and to all the haters that hated
you will see the vision of his song
Stay strong, we've got history
but it's still a mystery

I don't want to see life pass you by
I don't want to see a window of opportunity slip away
I don't want to see my brothers die
I cannot sit idly by and watch a grown man cry

To the broken men I love
I see your struggle
I see your fight within
but I know you've got the strength to win
and you will rise again from the ashes
like a Phoenix you will soar higher than ever before

Your Love

There is a coldness you have
inside of you
You built up a wall
and don't let people get through

I know deep in my heart
you are a good man scared
to face the truth

Open up, knock down that wall
I'm trying to break through
I'm screaming out to you

I promise I won't hurt you
I wrote this song for you, I love you
Why do you think I'm still here for you?

I'm not asking you to move a mountain
All I'm asking for is your love
that I know you have deep inside you

I can melt away your fears
and the wall of ice around you
if only you'd give me the chance
Won't you, please, take a stance
and let me in?

I'm tire of being on the outside
Looking in

Torn

I'm so torn
a part of me says to stay
another part of me says
to walk away

I'm teetering on the edge
screaming out
I have so much to say
with enough emotions to break
Will you catch me if I fall?

Thought this little girl inside me
had grown up but I have realized
just how much her heart is cut

Bleeding with broken wings
Will she ever find a dove of peace
to heal her wounds?

Teetering on the edge
crying out
I have so much to show
with enough emotion to glow
Will you catch me if I fall?

I'm so torn
a part of me says to stay
but another part of me says
to walk away

Trauma

I have been in the darkness with you
but I cannot stay in this sunken place
I cannot see my light through the drama
I have no choice but to walk away
to save myself from the trauma

I have lost my smile
I miss the warmth of the sunlight on my face
As this darkness envelopes us
We drift further and further apart
While it strips us of our hearts
No till death do us part

So much left unspoken
too much misunderstood
Please come with me
and get out of the hood

Maybe someday we will heal
and remove the face masks we all hide behind
pretending to be someone or something we're not
and begin to feel

Relationships

Relationships
What does love have to do with it?
Sometimes, it's not about love
Sometimes, it's about learning your next life lesson!

Love Verses Hate

Truth can come from both sources of love and hate
The question is this
Do you want the truth coming from a place of hate
or do you want the truth coming from a place of love?

The choice is yours, take your pick

Will we ever reach a higher level of consciousness?

When you bring truth through hate
then the road you travel will lead you to hate
but if you bring truth through love
then the road you travel will lead you to love
a higher level of consciousness

Don't we want to get hate out of this world?
If yes, then we must get rid of all hate
and embrace all love

Wake up world!

Don't hate them teach them
Don't judge them love them
Don't fear them show them
Don't separate them embrace them!

The ABC's Of Love Is

Love is awareness
Love is bittersweet
Love is blind
Love is caring
Love is communication
Love is compromise
Love is dreams
Love is emotions
Love is expression
Love is feeling
Love is foolish
Love is forever
Love is forgiving
Love is friendship
Love is giving
Love is happiness
Love is honesty
Love is joy
Love is kind
Love is letting go (the art of…)
Love is lonely
Love is memories
Love is nice
Love is open
Love is patience
Love is peace
Love is perseverance
Love is powerful
Love is respect
Love is sacrifice
Love is showing

Love is sincere
Love is togetherness
Love is trust
Love is unconditional
Love is unfair
Love is vulnerability
Love is warmth
Love is God (is love)
Love is you!

Night Might As Well Be Day

(copyright1956Lynn"jiji"Toliver)

Each night was always loving
when you were near to me
you went away
and left a blue memory
your love I cherish in vain

Must I go on this way
now that you're gone
night might as well be day

Don't need the stars
oh how I wish
that the darkness would never fall
What good's the moon?
What good am I dear
when I don't hear your call?
Oh how I miss you, dear heart

Each lonely hour I pray
now that you're gone
night might as well be day

*this is a song my late paternal grandmother wrote, I included it, along with the next entry, in my book to showcase where I get my writing abilities from, R.I.P. Bertha D.L. Gadson Toliver Hill aka jiji

Speak To Me Darling

(Bertha Toliver)

Verse
I may forget the sweetness of your kiss
Time may erase the warmth of your embrace
But these little things you say
They linger, linger from day to day

Chorus
Darling, kiss me, caress me
But speak to me
Please say these words
I long to hear
Although you love me by these sweet things you do
Heaven is when you speak to me

Verse (by Dana Toliver)
God guide him gently by my side
Let the soft winds blow my way
And the cool breeze touch my face
Warm my heart with his sweet embrace

Chorus
Darling, kiss me, caress me
But speak to me
Whisper those words
I long to hear
Although you love me by these sweet things you do
Heaven is when you speak to me

Queen

There is a special place
I have in my heart
where no other man has been
reserved only for a King
deserving of a Queen
who is willing to love you
unconditionally
and accepts you as you are
completely

There is no other
more caring
more loving
more giving
and more worthy than me

So let me be your angel
your one and only
Always and forever

Can't you see, if I could
I would give to you
the sun, the moon
and all the stars
Make me your Queen
and together
we will light up the sky

There is no greater love
than two hearts
beating as one
that is you and I
and someday, maybe
there will be…

Two souls coming
together connecting
like a magnetic force

The power of love
of a King and Queen
never before seen

There is a special place
I have in my heart
where no other man has been
deserving of this Queen
who loves you, unconditionally
accepts you as you are
completely
reserved only for you

Trust in me
and have faith in knowing
I will never do you wrong
Till the end of all time
Forever we will be strong!

Love And Fear

Love and fear
the only two emotions that exist
all negative emotion comes from fear
all positive emotion comes from love

In religion they teach to fear God
but isn't God love?
so if you are fearing God
then you are fearing love
and we are love
which means we are God
which means we are fearing ourselves

Because people have been taught to fear
when they see love they fear it and run away
and most no longer recognize it
even when it's staring them in the face

We were never meant to fear anything
and love and fear cannot exist simultaneously
so if you are fearing anything
you are incapable of loving anything

Erase the fear and embrace the love

Love is what we are
and it is the only truth!

Beauty Of The Sun

I see the beauty of the sun
Although the darkness comes
I see the beauty of the earth and the universe
Although I see the curse

I feel the love of everyone
Although hearts break
I feel the warmth of the sun
Shining down on everyone
I feel the loving arms of mother earth
Embracing every one of us

I see the beauty of the sun
Although the darkness comes
I see the beauty of the earth and the universe
Although I see the curse

I know the rays of the sun
Will light the way and brighten up your day
I know the power of the universe
Can bring us to heaven
I know the love of everyone
Will mend all broken hearts

I see the beauty of the sun
Although darkness comes
I see the beauty of the earth and the universe
Despite the curse, in the end

I know Love, thy will be done!

Fear Not, Love All

Fear not, love all then freedom will follow
and then you will reach a higher level tomorrow
but only if you follow your instincts and intuition
that inner voice inside you that allows you to feel
if something is right or wrong for you
but what is right for you
may not be what is right for someone else
and what is right for someone else
may not be what is right for you!

SECTION TWO

MASK

Mask

There you sit waiting
for your curtain call
when it's time
you slip on your mask
go out on stage
and play your part

At the end you take a bow
and disappear
behind the curtains
to remove the mask
you've just fooled the crowd with

No one suspects it's all an act
it's simply routine and that's a fact

Everyday
before you walk out your door
you put on this mask
a mask of deception
you wear all day

It's like a wall you build
one brick at a time

Only after the doors
are locked behind you
can you remove this mask
Only then can that wall come down
safe and sound

You can't go on this way,
for you know you are living a lie
knowing you can never be you
makes you want to break down and die

Day after day you find a way
to crack a smile
but only you know
that behind the mask
you are crying inside
a cry so deep you know
you will never be heard

Solid as a rock
you always seem
but only you know
who you should have become
isn't who you became

You became something
you're not

A mold of perfection
you no longer can live by

It's time to make a change
no more pretending to be
someone or something
you're not!

C.R.A.Z.Y. (I Am Who I Am)

They call me crazy
I can't be me
so it makes me that way

Can't believe I fell for you
I guess I am a little crazy

I am who I am

So why must I get treated
like an outcast?

Don't feel like I belong
to this world

Where do I fit in?

Never been accepted
for who I truly am

So I **C**reatively **R**each **A**nd **Z**estfully **Y**earn
for my dreams

Call me C.R.A.Z.Y.!

I'm glad I am who I am
I'm glad I'm me!

Ever-Changing Winds

I flow like the ever-changing winds blow
mild at times, calm, peaceful and timid
but once angered gusts will blow, strong, hard and fast
like the ever-changing winds blow, I flow

Look To The Core

Look to the core
to know and understand
who I really am

Look to the core
and you shall find
a unique, warm-hearted
caring and knowledgable soul
yet, with a spirit
that's been forever scarred

To understand me
and to know who I really am
just look to the core deep within

Ambiguous

I've never felt like I have ever been
able to fit in, always pretending
everything's okay
with the anguish never subsiding

I'm ready to fly to a place in the sky
where I can be free to just be me

I know the way it feels to be
so ambiguous, stuck in hell
alone on my own, tormented
with no end in sight, too broken to run
feeling distraught

I feel the numbness setting in
the chaos and confussion
of what it feels like to be
so ambiguous

Too Blind To See

I couldn't see
that I've always been free

Free to be me
Free to just be

I was too blind to see
to be all you can be
and for your spirit to soar
you must face the darkness
you have deep inside

It's the only way
you will see the light

I was too blind to see
that I've always been free

Free to be me
Free to just be!

Born Like Me

Some are born with a destiny
meant to make history

And some are born like me
with a destiny full of mystery

Nowhere

G-Mix
It's been a merry-go-round
round and round we go
when will we stop, nobody knows

Dray
It was a roller coaster ride
that led to nowhere
but a path of destruction

Thanks for the ride
but it is time for me to get off
and leave it all behind

It is time for me to find a better ride
one that will lead to my destiny
to all my dreams I have inside of me

Through The Storm

How many storms must I walk through
before I get a breakthrough?
The journey is long and although I get weary
I must stay strong

How many times is the rain going to fall?
The tides are rising
The strength it takes to wade through the raging waters
Takes the strength of an army of men
Will I ever make it through?
Will I ever win?

My light is dimming
and the darkness has covered me
smothering me, I need air
Does anyone care?

Maybe someday they will see my light
and see the damage they have done and rescue me?
Until then I must weather the storm, alone

Family Secrets

Family secrets
taken to the grave
none were brave enough to face
the power of truth and grace

The shame more powerful
than the gain of freedom
they would have felt
from the burden lifted off their hearts

Family secrets
spreading from generation to generation
like a cancer spreading through your veins

The regrets more powerful
than the freedom they could have known
from a burden of weight carried
far too long, lifted

Family secrets
taken to the grave
none were brave enough to face
the power of truth and grace

And the power of love
they would have known
had they spoken the truth

Rose Petals

One long-stemmed rose
Perfect in its beauty
The winds, how they blew
One by one petals began to fall
Until there was nothing
Nothing left but the stem
With all its thorns

One Kind Of Mother

(February 24, 2012)

The three C's:
    Controls (they can be extremely controlling)
    Criticizes (they can be overly critical)
    Counts (they tend to keep track of their "gifts")

Other possible descriptive attributes:

Judgemental
Shows Favoritism
Materialistic
Self-centered
Neglectful
Lacks Empathy
Anxious
Lives in Denial
Defensive
Co-Dependent
Selfish
Impulsive
Demanding
Impatient
Manipulative
Inconsiderate
Hypocritical
Narcissistic
Passive-Aggressive
Skewed Value System
Emotionally Disconnected
Non-Attentive

Loves Conditionally
Functions as an Addict:

    examples: Alcoholic/Drugs
            Work-o-holic
            Shop-o-holic
            Food-o-holic

My Father's Son

If my own father couldn't love me
why should any other man love me?

This is my reminder
that I was supposed to be my father's son

One Kind Of Father

(June 22, 2016)

Absent!
Secretive
Self-Centered
Neglectful
Passive-Aggressive
Deceitful
Dishonest
Hypocritical
Defensive
Selfish
Manipulative
Lives in Denial
Emotionally Disconnected
Not Authentic (the great pretender)
Functions as an Addict:

    examples: Alcoholic/Drugs
        Work-o-holic
        Sex-o-holic
        Food-o-holic

A Promise Made

When her mother fell ill twenty seven years ago
why did she go and make a promise
that would eventually lead to our demise?

Failing to protect us
from the abuse her mother gave
she couldn't see her mother's ways

Put on the back burner
left there to simmer
we were second in line
she turned on a dime
and left us behind

This is such a sad song
because of a promise
made to God, she kept

Should'a, Would'a, Could'a

Questions
What could have been done?
What should have been done?

Answers
Could have taken heed to my warnings
Should have fixed and removed the problems
Instead of just sweeping them under the rug
And covering them up
If I were you, I would have listened
To my words of wisdom

Could have face the mirror
Should have come out of denial
And resolved your own anxiety issues
If I were you, I would not have taken me for granted
Or turned and walked away

Could have been daddy's little girl
Should have known a mother's love
Of support and guidance
If I were you, I would have taken me with you
And not left me behind
And if I were you, I would not have chosen
My mother, first, over my child

Through all the coldness, I found warmth
Through all the neglect, I found my strength
And even though it was a private hell
That I lived in, I wish you all well

Just A Dream

A family gathering
Under the night sky
One by one
Each spoke their truth
But when it was your turn to speak
Everyone began to disperse
As usual
You're the ambiguous one
You turn away
As the rain falls on your face
Then a stranger appears
And for the first time
You are seen
For the first time
You are heard
But then you wake to realize
It was all just a dream
You have awoken
To the nightmare of your soul
Trapped inside a darkened hole
In the mist of the storm
There you sit, alone
Wanting to be seen
Like a phoenix rising
You want to break free
And go home to dream

Sad To Know

I hope, someday, you finally see us
and see the sunshine in our eyes

It is sad to know
you will journey to the other side
not knowing us or believing in us
the way you do her

I hope, someday, you will face the mirror
and see yourself as you, truly, are

It is sad to know
you will see the other side
without seeing us in a positive light
or respecting us as you do her

I hope, someday, you can learn
to accept us for who we, really, are
with all of our uniquenesses and differences
before you say your goodbye

It is sad to know you will leave this world
Not seeing the good in us because of
a mother's love who sealed our fate
I hope you wake up before it's too late!

Dear Family

Dear family, don't you see
our destiny's embedded in me?

Grown numb to the pain
of being locked away with the shame
and there's no one to blame

Encaged, I feel the rage burning inside

Moments turn into hours
hours turn into days
and days turn into nights

My only escape is to fall into my dreams
and pretend I'm free from the misery
of this destiny that's been placed upon me

But it's only a dream
the reality of my destiny soon sinks in
as I awake to realize that I'm still alive

Forced to keep the secrets, yet, another day
I face the pain and the shame
as the burning rage builds inside
until I'm ill, too ill to feel
anyone or anything, I want to scream

Enough is enough!

Don't wake me up from my dreams
sleep is the only freedom that I know

Wrapped Up

You are too busy wrapped up
into how everything looks
and appears to look

But that's not what matters

It's what's on the inside
it's what is in your heart
that truly matters

You have never been able to see
past the cover, past the shell

Can't see the real me!

You are to busy wrapped up
into yourself to open your eyes
to the truth that stares you in the face

You can't see the real me!

Closed In

It's a double edge sword
I face day after day
Damned if I do
Damned if I don't
Too selfish of you
To step outside of yourself
Forced to enter into your world
Never knowing which one
Of your two faces will appear
The passive or aggressive one
That manipulates everyone
Harboring adolescent fears
Unable to show any tears
With the functional mentality
Of an addict unable to relinquish control
With your un-empathetic soul
All that stuff festering inside you
Too frightened to speak the truth
That bond you so long for
Fades into obscurity
All the words left unsaid
Simmering on the edge
Finally boils over
Left all alone by those not concerned
Having to protect myself
From getting burned
I was forced to grow up too soon
Oppressed from my youth
Never knowing the truth
Taught to be emotionless
Don't want to rock the boat

So I pretend and put up a front
I stay away to keep my sanity
Buried deep within
Is your world so closed in

Private Hell

Forever imprisoned
In a private hell
With no one to come home to
And no one to hold you

The only company you keep
Is the radio and T.V.
Empty space resides between the walls
No ringing of a telephone
No knock at your door

No one's there to catch you
When you fall
The only thing there
Is a stuffed teddy bear

Throw a penny in a well
And wish upon a fairy tale
To escape this empty space
And you know, know on cares
That you are forever imprisoned
In a private hell

Seed

When a baby is born
when that seed is planted
if you don't nurture that baby
when its born, its spirit won't grow
and its soul dies

It's just like a seed
you plant in the ground
if you don't water it, it won't grow

I feel like that seed still in the ground
waiting for someone to come by
and water it so it can grow

I'm still waiting for someone
to come along and nurture my soul
so I can grow and my spirit can blossom
like that sed in the ground
waiting to be watered

In My Eyes

They say the eyes are the window to one's soul
So why can't they see the pain in my eyes,
see my broken soul and see that I'm no longer whole?

I am battered and bruised, left to bleed
as they watch this butterfly lose her wings
unable to fly with just one wing

You see in my eyes, my dreams have died
and faded away into the night sky
Now all that is left is the moonlight
And memories of what I can never be

Just look into these eyes of mine
There you will find this butterfly
There you will see this heart of mine

Unable to fly with just one wing
I can no longer be free
and be who I am supposed to be

To Be Gone

So, here you sit feeling all alone
can't wait for the day you'll be sent home
that day you will be laid to rest
can't fathom why it's taking so long

To be gone

At times you wish the day was near
for you know you have nothing to fear
but, to cross over, you must pass through the light
burning however bright
blinding as it may seem, it's like a dream

To be gone

At times you wish the day was near
for you know you have nothing to fear
God, only, knows when that day will come
when you close your eyes to forever sleep
so you can rest in peace

To be gone

At times you wish the day was here
for you know you have nothing at all to fear
oh, how you wish to fly
free as the wind, free as a butterfly
like angels floating in the sky high above the clouds

To be gone

At times you wish the day was near
for you know you have nothing to fear

To be gone

The Other Side

Why was I sent back to this place?
It was so peaceful on the other side
Why would anyone choose to live in this world
when there is another world that exist?

A world of peace, love, happiness
compassion and empathy
A world where hate, greed, selfishness
dishonesty and violence does not exist

This world I know, this world I have seen
this world where I once was so happy and carefree

But the only way to get there
is to go through the darkness
A space that most have been taught to fear

Now, how do I get back to the other side
to this place of peace that I call Paradise
without leaving her behind
to suffer in this world that so cold and cruel?

I just can't wait to go home to the other side

Not Of This World

I am not of this place
I know I do not belong here
I know where home is
and it is not of this world
It's all just temporary
my mold illness will take my life
and it was one hundred percent preventable
had I known the truth

Yes, I get angry sometimes
and have every right to cry
because this is not how I wanted to go home
But I know there is a lesson here
that has yet to be learned

The lyrical reminder from Mariah of Psalms 129:2
"They have greatly oppressed me from my youth
but they will not gain victory over me"
goes out to all those I wish well

Until I make it home, until the world makes it home
I'll keep prayer in my heart for everyone
for I am the one who carries all the emotional weight
that's too heavy a load to bear

Perhaps I am a fallen angel sent here to learn
or an angel sent here to teach and guide
rose petals from the lure of this world

Only with God from within do I muster the strength to go on
because I am not of this world, I'm beyond it!

What Will It Take

What will it take for them to see
the change in your heart?

Going through all the pain helped you to grow
like that seed in the ground, the rain falls
but after the rain is gone sprouts the bud of a flower

What will it take for them to see
you have come out of your cocoon?

Like a butterfly you grew wings
now you can soar to the moon
to the stars and the sun
high up in the sky, you will fly

What will it take for them to let you go
to grow into a flower that's in full bloom?

To love you enough to set you free
to fly like the butterfly you want to be
nurture yourself and they will see
you can be all you can be

So, what will it take to open your heart
and let the love and the light shine in?

Superwoman

Everyone expects me to be
this super-human person
but when I can't
live up to that title
everyone looks at me
with disappointment
and they pass judgments

I am only human
I can't be superwoman
anymore

I make mistakes
like everybody else
but the only difference is
my mistakes are not forgiven
nor are they forgotten

I did not choose
to come to this world
nor did I choose my family
my family chose me
this world chose me

Now how can they expect me
to be super-human

They've got to understand
I am only human
I can't be superwoman
anymore

Rose Tinted Eyes

Can't see your own delusions
through your distorted view
with your rose tinted eyes
only you can despise
your own self image

The denial of your reflection
runs deep
the lack of respect you show
with the cutting words you speak
and no empathy in sight
you must be emotionally weak

Scarred for life you can't see me
for who I truly am
you look straight through me
with those rose tinted eyes

Can't see how you
offend those around you
with your disillusioned thoughts of reality
and your unrealistic demands
when confronted you take a defensive stand

Let go of the control
the dark deep secrets you keep
has sown what you reap

Passing the blame
the conversations go up in flames
as you watch me burn down to the ground
with your rose tinted eyes, only you can despise
I feel the hatred inside

I hide to keep from
losing my mind
how can someone
be so blind?
Where is your humanity?
I have found my
inner peace and want
to keep my sanity

So I'm letting go
letting go of the hope
and the fantasy
that you will ever see me
clearly through your
rose tinted eyes

Angel Of Me

Sweet angel of me
I'm speaking to you my inner child
don't you cry or run away
and leave us all behind

Sweet angel of me
don't allow the world
to break you down
someday, it will all turn around

Though the burdens you carry
are too heavy a load for you to hold
sweet angel of me, hold on
and you will see a new dawn

Sweet angel of me
face the fears they want to run and hide from
and pretend not to see
too scared to face the mirror
and feel the pain of yesteryear

Nobody knows all the pain
hidden deep inside
soon you will see the sun rise
darkness falls before the dawn, hold on

Sweet angel of me, stay strong

Reflection

So many pieces left shattered
on the ground
Every step you take
you're cut on broken glass
longing for things to last
but you must learn to let go of the past

Thought you could not move on
but you saw an angel in the reflection
of the broken glass
You turn to look and see wings growing on your back
and found the strength to pick up the pieces
of the shattered glass

That moment you saw your reflection
you realized the battle is done, the war is won
and there has always been an angel
carrying you

And you realized the angel was you!

Gemini

What all Gemini's need to do is
Find, Accept, Embrace then Master
their twin self

Unknown

Gemini's live where dreams are reality
and where reality itself is a dream

Just as fire needs oxygen to survive
love needs freedom to flourish

If you don't stand for something
you will fall for anything

Simply Complex

I'm a simple person
but sometimes simplicity
can be very complex

D.A.D.

This is the story of a six year old girl name **A**ngel
and a nine year old boy named **D**amon
trapped inside a twenty-one year old named **D**iamond

Angel, so sweet, so innocent, so alone
in her own shy, quiet, little world
and Damon longing for attention
confused and frightened about what's yet to come

Here is Diamond scared of Angel
never knowing when she will appear, so subtly

Damon gets jealous and angry
so he throws tantrums
to get attention whenever he can

This is the story of Diamond's life, my life!

The Definition Of D.A.D.

Three becomes one

Diamond	Angel	Damon
Optimistic	Pessimistic	Neutral
Sensible	Gullible	Self-absorbed
Adult	Child-like	Adolescent
Thirty something	Age six	Age nine
Level-headed	Needs guidance	Seeks approval
Happy	Unhappy	Angry
Assertive	Passive	Aggressive
High self-esteem	Low self-esteem	Self-destructive
High self-worth	Low self-worth	Selfish
See the good	Only sees the bad	Only sees himself
Under control	Never in control	Controlling
Warm	Abandoned by father	Neglected by mother
Logical	Sweet	Demands attention
Rational	Playful	Jealous
Free-spirited	Impatient	Rebellious
Nice	Curious	Cold
Flirtatious	Sensitive	Irritable
Caring	Caring	Unpredictable
Loving	Bright	Loud
Empathetic	Quiet	Unorganized
Patient	Insecure	Closed-minded
Organized		Irrational
Open-minded		Intolerant
Giving		Quick-witted
Tolerant		Uncaring
Artistic		Insecure
Humanitarian		
Intellectual		
Talkative		
Secure		

Lightbulb Moment

By defining D.A.D. I came to the realization that many people have a form of narcissism; judges, doctors, lawyers, politicians, celebrities, etc. I believe there is a little part of all of us who wants to be the center of attention; who wants to be in control. But, even, if it's not narcissism we possess, perhaps, it's egotism and the mentality that the world revolves around us; the Damon in me, perhaps, the Damon in all of us. It's an all about me attitude to the detriment of everyone around you. A deep selfishness that doesn't know any other way to exist.

I have realized that most people have a Damon in them. At some point in time many people have been stuck in an adolescent phase of development and never mature into actual adulthood. I believe many people get stuck in different phases in their lives at different times in their lives. I believe this is the reason why so many so-called adult relationships fail. An adult dating an adolescent or a child is just wrong. Adults know how to take responsibility for their actions, however, adolescents and children don't.

I, also, believe many people have an Angel in them; the child Phase of development. The phase we will all one day revert back to before we die. A child looks up to anyone who is older. An adult and an adolescent can control a child which is why an adult child in a relationship with an adult or adolescent adult never works. Here is an example:

> My ex-husband thought he would be able to "mold" me into who he wanted me to be because at that time, he was in his adolescent phase and I was in my child phase but I quickly grew into

my adolescent phase and moved on. Like most adolescents, I hated being controlled.

Adolescents like to be in control and control others, however, they also need guidance which is why a lot of adolescent adults seek out adults in relationship: the father figure or the mother figure they never had and are in search of. However, once the adolescent adult grows into adulthood that adult is no longer needed and the relationship fails. And a child adult with an adult is just creepy.

Since most adults never make it to adulthood most people do not realize that they are not, actually, dealing with their adult partners or their adult parents or friends. They are, actually, dealing with an adult who is more like a child or adolescent teen. I have realized, now, that I was never living with an adult mother but was, actually, living with an adolescent mother. I can, clearly, see, now, the problem with my mother having to take care of her ailing mother, who had reverted back to a child phase of life. It was like putting an eleven year old, adolescent, my mother, in charge of a three year old child, her mother.

By defining D.A.D. and discovering the Damon in me, I have realized that I have just defined the majority of most adults in the world. How depressing. No wonder society is so messed up. It is being run by a bunch of spoiled adolescent adults. I see, now, that just because you make it to be an adult doesn't mean you make it to adulthood.

Who Am I?

Am I an optimist or a pessimist?
From what I have been told I'm always fair weather
With a zest to take on the world with confidence
Overly optimistic, at times, not keeping in mind
That life, sometimes, just, isn't fair

Do I follow my heart or follow my head?
I'm a happy medium, head first type of mind
Sentimental as the next girl
But I try not to let my emotions get the best of me
The trouble is, what seems sensible
May not always be what is right for me

How thoughtful am I?
They say I'm thoroughly thoughtful, normally nice
A genuinely considerate girl who knows what empathy is
However, I'm not always miss manners
But I'm not Attila the Hun, either
I may say the wrong things, sometimes
But my heart is in the right place
Even when my mouth is not

So True

How do I approach life? I wing it!

However, I am strongly committed to humanitarian issues and social improvements. I am, extremely, aware of the interconnection and interdependence of all people; I relate personal issues to something greater than myself and I see the ramifications of personal actions, plus, I wish to contribute something of value to the world.

The ideals of equity, fairness and human rights are ingrained into the fabric of my character. I am, truly, interested in the good of the whole and I am, rarely, focused on my own personal well-being; I tend to overlook my own personal needs, desires and feelings.

I have very little patience for conservative narrow-mindedness and consider myself a "global citizen" and would rather not claim a narrow, limited identification based on race, ethnicity and heritage; I am considered to be friendly and express a kind, impersonal, good-will towards others which affords me many acquaintances but, preferably, very few, really, close friends.

I rarely show my emotions, but I will cry at a commercial; I prefer to stay on the rational side of life even though I am an Empath and carry the emotions of the world inside me; I literally, feel the world's emotions every second of every day

I am fiercely independent, to a point, and refuse to be possessed or controlled by anyone; I am, in many ways, an eternal playful child with a bright mind who grasps ideas quickly and tend to have a multitude of interests and dislike limiting myself to focus on just one, I very much loathe repetition, however, I'm aware that within this book I have repeated myself, I'm only human

I am a people watcher, an observer, and need mental stimulation every bit as much as I need food and drink; communication is a key factor and many have said that I have a talent for speaking and writing, go figure.

I have a rather light and mischievous sense of humor and, rarely, take anything too seriously; and although I crave emotional involvement I am, frequently, unwilling to commit myself to anything or limit my personal freedom and mobility.

My Life Story

It's like I am standing outside in the middle of a snowstorm with no coat, no shoes, and no shelter from the storm. There I stand looking inside seeing everyone sitting by the fire where it's nice and warm, laughing and having a good time. They look outside the window and see me standing there yet, they don't care to invite me in or even come outside to offer me a coat. I knock at the door then they answer and say, "sorry, there's nothing I can do for you" so I leave to go find shelter somewhere else, yet everywhere I go I get refused. No one cares enough to open their door or offer me a coat. Everyone pretends like they cannot see me, standing there, looking at them through their window; they act like I do not exist.

    Nobody seems to understand that I've been used, I've been abused and felt so confused, I've been pushed aside and victimized, I have felt invisible and been miserable. I have been mistreated, but I have never been defeated.

My Life Story Continued

Wounded Dove

And the story continues with Angel, a little girl, who grew up very sheltered but wise beyond her years. She had always known, early on, she was ambiguous and always felt out of place. She knew she would be traveling a rough road, alone and unguided, thrown into a world divided.

She has always carried the weight of the world on her shoulders but muddled through the tears and fears while dreaming of what she could be; wading in insecurities. She, still, feels like a child who grew up too soon, longing for stability. Is there such a thing as a perfect family?

As she grew, she gravitated towards a patriarch to save her from the misery. So many turned on her and sold her out while that knife chipped away at her. All she could do is sit by and watch life pass her by. She learned to grow numb to the madness and block it all away but never able to feel stable and free. On the verge of dying, she almost slipped away and knows she missed a lot of life along the way.

With her Guardian Angels by her side, she managed to face the world and keep her soul alive.

Someone To Love

Longing, searching, hoping, and praying for some answers, she realized that all she really wants it to matter to someone and to be validated and loved.

The love of family, friends and others has always been elusive. It seems as though, ever since she was four years old, there's always been a black cloud hovering over her; maybe even a curse that follows her. She feels like her voice was silenced and her heart was chained.

Guidance

Looking back, she realized the one thing that was missing, throughout her life, was guidance. She always had to guide herself through all the pain and sorrow. She waited for someone to find her and remember she was left standing outside in the snowstorm but no one found her and now that little girl is grown.

Friendship

The little girl growing up was never able to make many friends out of fear they would use that knife and chip away at her as her family had done. But now, grown, the importance of friendship hits home.

Isolation

Frozen in fear, scared of the world and getting her heart broken, she sits in isolation wishing she was free. She knows she has been mentally and physically locked away being neglected, abandoned and abused. She wanted to break out of her shell, but she needed guidance because she knew on the inside of that shell she was as soft as a feather and scared she would blow away.

To Carry On

Fragile and frail, and always with her outer shell, she managed to carry on but deep in her heart there would always be a place of longing to find what she's been dreaming of; love, peace and happiness.

Handwriting Analysis

(written by Carlos Pedregal, 1990)

Well-Bred and Educated:
You are well-bred. Your unswerving corrections in all circumstances makes you an exceptional colleague, companion or friend.

Temporary Discouragement:
Your handwriting reveals that at the time you wrote this analysis you were experiencing a feeling of discouragement. Your feeling could be the result of a recent incident that has had a definite effect upon you.

Respect for Human Beings:
This feature is an outstanding characteristic of your personality. Respect for other human beings is at the core of the concept of love, friendship, and freedom.

Family Disagreement:
Situations you have lived through during your childhood have left their stamp on your character. You have not developed all the aspects of your personality as a result of the conditioning you received in your family. Your handwriting clearly shows that problems within the family caused you great deal of suffering. The effects of this suffering remain with you, slightly affecting you, even now.

Altruism:
Your regard and consideration for other people before yourself has a tendency to involve you in difficult situations. You continue your altruistic behavior even though

you understand that the beneficiaries of altruism rarely understand it and rewards are seldom commensurate with generosity.

Sociable:

You are a gentle and likable person, true signs of a good upbringing, and your kindness and amiability don't prevent you from being determined and energetic. Your good breeding does not prevent you from achieving your aims; in fact, it helps you attain them in far more agreeable ways than those employed by most people.

Active:

You are an active and efficient person. Your handwriting displays a great vitality and a good capacity for work. If one entrusts you with any kind of task you will carry it through successfully.

My Filing Cabinet Brain Memory Recall Analogy

An average person's brain:

Nice, neat files stored
in filing cabinets
that are labeled throughout
different sections of the brain
for easier recall and memory

Note:

Filing cabinets take up more space
therefore, less information can be
stored, however

My brain:

Filing cabinets have been removed
to store more information but since
there are no cabinets to store the files
they are stored wherever there is room
in the brain to put them which makes
memory recall a little more challenging

Bottom line:

Less information better stored
as opposed to more information
stored jumbled

Everything Changes (Clean Version)

I'll never forget what's been done
Everything changes in time
Letting go and saying goodbye is never easy
The last tangible piece of a legacy, gone forever
It's such a tragedy

It may not mean anything to you
But it means everything to me, don't you see?
I tried to stop the train from crashing
To avoid the heartbreak and devastating losses
But I was always met with resistance

I want to break down and cry
But if I do I won't ever stop until the end of time
So let the chips fall where they may
There's nothing more left to say
It's too late to stop history from repeating itself
I see another train wreck coming

The impact of the choices made
And the legacy that's being left today
Can never be undone

Now all that's left is hope and faith
To change everything back to the way it was
Perhaps, this will be a blessing in disguise
Only time will tell if things turn out well

In The Mirror

'The art of letting go'
is about letting go
of who I used to be

The girl in the mirror
I no longer see

The dancer in me
I had to grieve

In the mirror
who do I see
staring back at me?

A black butterfly
with broken wings!

Mycotoxicosis

I'll never forget that day
sitting in my doctor's office
when he told me the news
I was so confused

I'm knock, knock, knockin'
on heaven's door
What for?
Myalgic Encephalomyelitis
Am I strong enough
to get through this?
Will I make it through
this rain with so much pain?
With no cure in sight
I must not give up the fight

Literally,
from the tips of your toes
to the top of your head
you feel like you're
the walking dead

You wish you could be
put out of your misery
to be poisoned by
mycotoxins
is such a travesty

At times it lies dormant inside
until something comes along
and wakes it up again
to reek havoc in your body
causing your life to be disrupted
and turned upside down
sometimes lasting for several
months at a time

There are better days but
mostly you have bad days
and even those days where
you, literally, feel like
you're dying, suffocating!
If I could just breathe
through this

So many things left undone
if only I had the freedom
but for those who don't
comprehend it, I put up a
front and grin and bear it

I'm humbled by the power,
will, strength and pure
stubbornness of this illness
the amount of pain and fatigue
of this disease is simply
unbearable and
incomprehensible!

What I have learned through
all of this is that there are
many who are twisted
and sick, I have been
woken up to the reality of
society that we are not all
human, we are not the Elite
race, some of us have fallen
from grace

Journeys

Through many journeys and avid soul searching
I have discovered, learned, realized and accepted
that I will never be able to live up to nor will I succumb
to the expectations, standards and pressures
of my family and society

So to any who pass judgments on me
or looks down upon me in any way, I would say to you
be thankful that you don't ever have to walk a day in my
shoes so you will never, truly, know, understand or see
all that I am!

Pseudo Mutuality

I never realized the amount of damage all the emotional and psychological abuse I suffered from within the narcissistic environment I grew up in caused, until I got into a situation with someone who I thought was a good friend. He turned out to be equally as damaging as all the other addicts, narcissists, psychopaths, and sociopaths I have encountered throughout my life. It has, not only, been devastating, hurtful, and paralyzing, but it triggered my PTSD.

PTSD is something I have lived with since I was nine years old. I fell back into this dark place I was in for nine years of my life from the age of nine to eighteen when I took steps to end my life. I wound up in a coma for two days, and yet my mother was clueless as to what actually happened. My PTSD was triggered later when I got the diagnosis of my chronic illness, called mycotoxicosis, back in 2005.

I was always aware from the time I was four years old that my life would not be easy and that there were some serious problems within my family and this world, but I was just a child. Being the youngest in the household, I learned to follow the status quo, which was to stay silent, keep to myself, and keep up appearances, never allowing the outside world in; otherwise, the world would figure out just how dysfunctional things really were and still are. I was silenced to the point that I, literally, did not speak for almost five years. The silence for me became deafening. I learned to keep my emotions to myself but that led me to become a ticking time bomb, and at age eighteen, I exploded!

As if that wasn't bad enough, to have to experience abuse and trauma from my grandmother and then feel responsible for the death of my grandfather when I was only nine years old for not speaking up before the tragic event occurred was devastating. I remember the day my sister and I were sat down and told that my grandfather shot my grandmother and then shot himself, killing himself, which triggered the onset of, what I later learned was, PTSD.

I was there, at my grandparent's house, the week before the horrific event happened. That was the night when I saw the gun and witnessed for the first time the extreme verbal abuse of my grandfather by my grandmother. I tried to intervene. I tried to stand up for my grandfather, but my grandmother turned her anger toward me.

The day my sister and I were told about my grandfather's passing was the only time anything was ever said to us, by my mother, about the tragic event. It was already well established that we were not to talk about it. It was buried like everything else. We must keep up the facade of a normal family so much that my mother had the tragedy kept out of all news media. We were to carry on like it never happened, but I carried the guilt of knowing that I could have saved my grandfather's life if, only, I had spoken up about him having a gun. This guilt lingered until the day I swallowed four bottles of pills, on September 25, 1989.

My grandmother survived the shooting, and after she was released from the hospital, my mother brought her home to live with us. I was so confused; why would she come to live with us when she was so abusive to me, and she was the reason why my grandfather was dead? But that was my mother's mother, and my mother promised to take care of her, which came at the expense of my sister and me. We were always on the back burner. My grandmother took precedence, always. I began to realize my mother lived in this place called denial, and I began to speak up and became rebellious against the dysfunction and abusive nature of my grandmother.

For the next nine years, I live in this haze of dysfunction, abuse, neglect, and despair. I lived in a shell with secrets I wasn't allowed to share with the outside world. I grew numb to all the madness and the more I rebelled, the crazier they said I was. I knew I was considered the black sheep, the "troublemaker," and became the scapegoat. I could sense the resentment building up because I would stir the pot again and again. But after five years of not speaking, I vowed to never allow anyone to silence me, ever, again!

After my "suicide attempt" or as I call it my death experience, I spent my twenties soul-searching for who I am and how and where I fit in. I realized I was robbed of my childhood. I learned how to fake being happy, and I began looking for love in all the wrong places, desperately looking for anyone who could rescue me from my life. The only "love" I had ever known was so destructive and dysfunctional that I ended up gravitating toward what was familiar with every relationship I entered into. Dysfunction was all I knew so I sought out what I knew and became everyone's savior because I, too, needed saving.

This soul-searching journey that began in my twenties has continued; it has led me to write this book and has led me to where I am today. However, my journey is not over, and although I have made it through many obstacles, I still have a long journey ahead until I can fully heal emotionally, physically, psychologically, and spiritually from all the traumas and ill health I have suffered and endured throughout my life. And part of my healing process has been the discovery of, and acknowledgment of, my psychological and emotional abuse at the hands of my mother and now ex-friend. And even though I grew up in a toxic environment, and I have always been surrounded by toxic people and addicts, I, now, understand what a narcissist truly is.

SECTION THREE

INSIGHT

I Have Found My Light

To the disbelievers
to the unfaithful
against all odds
I have made it

Look at me now

I may not have
all the money
in the world, right now
but I have something
far more valuable

I have a beautiful daughter
who loves me unconditionally

I have found serenity
an inner peace
a light that shines, bright
inside of me
that no one can turn off
no one but me

I have found my light
and as long as I am alive
my light will shine on

I Am Human

I am neither
Republican nor Democrat
Liberal nor Conservative
Right Wing nor Left

I am neither
Catholic nor Jewish
Mormon nor Islamic
Baptist nor Methodist

I am neither
American nor Canadian
Russian nor Australian
African nor Asian

I am neither
Black nor White
Indian nor Mexican
Middle Eastern nor Italian

I am simply Human
who sheds the same blood
as my fellow Humans
half way around the world

This is why we are in the state we are in today
we have separated ourselves from one another
by putting all these labels on everything

What is the purpose of separating ourselves now?
We, as Humans, are all in this fight together
whether you accept that or not!

It saddens me to know
that I live in a nation that is
so divided, so heartless
and deceitful
and it saddens me to know
that I live in a world that is so
separated and cold

Selfishness and greed
are killing this world
and Satan has His hold
but I pray this world will
wake up someday
and realize the truth
and there is but only one
Truth…

And war is never the answer!

Words Of Wisdom

Listen to my words of wisdom
Let us not forget existentialism
I maybe only twenty-seven
But I can say I've been to heaven
Truth can be hard to fathom
And lies are often taken erroneously to heart
So, I ask the reprobates to look in the mirror and see the reciprocity
Listen to my words of wisdom
Open up your heart and mind, open up your eyes
And see the other side of wisdom!

The Light

We, as humans, have a disease
those of us who know, understand and can see
the light that has been cast upon us

To understand it there can be no hate, no greed,
no fear and no selfishness in your heart, mind and soul

I was given the chance to experience the light
It allowed me to see the other side of life

Though, here on Earth, most won't
ever get that chance to see the light
and to understand this disease
we all, as humans, possess

A disease of hate, fear, greed, selfishness
and heartlessness

Those of us who know, understand
that we have this disease and to cure it
you must allow love in and let the light within
shine bright then your mind and soul will be
at ease

Be the light and it shall set you free

Spirit Soul

If it is true that soul means life
and with life comes death
and if it is true that we are souls
and we, as humans, die
then would it not mean that the soul dies?

And if it is true that spirit means one's essence
and one's essence is one's energy
and if everything is energy
and energy never dissipates
it can only disperse
then would it not be true
that one's spirit never dies?

Is it true the spirit is housed in one's soul?

If it is true
that the spirit and soul are the same
then would it not be true
that one truly never dies
and that the soul continues on as a spirit?

Soul=Spirit=Energy=Power

Wisdom

Rise to a higher level of conscience
a higher level of knowledge called wisdom

Will we ever get there?
Will we ever reach wisdom?

Knowledge does not equal wisdom
it's just a stepping stone to reach it
we must go beyond

Until we understand that knowledge
is not the end of the road
then we will never reach wisdom
which means we will never reach
the ultimate truth
because in wisdom lies ultimate truth
which means we will never experience true love
because in ultimate truth lies true love

Spirituality Verses Religion

Spirituality is having faith in knowing there is something higher or greater than ourselves, the ego. Spirituality peals back the layers of religions and gets to the core of what they all have; a knowing that there is something greater than us, something beyond our own egos. I know that this something greater is love which connects us all together as one.

> If God is love
> and love is God
> and God is everything
> and everything is God
> and everything is energy
> and we are energy
> then we are everything
> we are God
> and we are love
> God lies within us
> God is not separate from us
> and if God is self
> and self is God
> then fear of God is fear of self
> fear of love and fear of everything
> and fear is a negative emotion
> so fear of anything creates negative emotions
> within ourselves, our psyche

There is a difference between being spiritual and being religious. You can be very religious yet not be spiritual, at all. Spirituality connects you to yourself; it is the relationship you have with the self. Religion is just ritual and routine. It teaches people to fear God, to fear the self, to fear death and to fear everything. It is a way to institutionalize faith and faith should never be labeled. Labeling limits you to what lies outside of that label. With spirituality you know and understand that the search for truth and answers lies within one's self and you do not need to search outside of yourself.

Ball And Chain

True freedom is endless and boundless!

Education
Healthcare
Medicine
Insurance
Religion
Media
Business
Military
Banking
Pharmaceuticals
Politics
Money
Laws

All these things keep us from reaching true freedom
True freedom is not linked to any of these things
We are all chained to these things and the only way to reach true freedom is to break the chains!

Insight

Is God your conscience?
Is your conscience God?

Is spirit your conscience?
Is conscience your spirit?

Will I wake up and see tomorrow?
Will I wake up tomorrow and see?

Have we forgotten about existentialism?

If you are living in fear
then you are not living
letting go of fear
is the key to freedom

Follow your heart, your instincts
and your intuition

And remember, just because
you have been taught something
doesn't always mean
that what you've been taught is correct

Don't assume information is true
just because it's coming
from a so-called creditable source

Don't accept information you receive as factual
just because it's coming
from an elder or an authority figure

We all have the power to free ourselves
so free yourself!

Choices

You are guided to make choices
that align with your destiny that was
pre-written and pre-planned
before you were ever born

Quotes

"Today's mighty oak is just yesterday's nut that held its ground."

-David Icke

"Just look at us. Everything is backwards; everything is upside down. Doctors destroy health, lawyers destroy justice, universities destroy knowledge, governments destroy freedom, the major media destroy information and religions destroy spirituality."

-Michael Ellner

"Many are destined to reason wrongly, others, not to reason at all; and others, to persecute those who do reason."

-Voltaire

"Planet Earth is the asylum to which the rest of the universe sends its lunatics."

-Voltaire

"The mysteries of life speak to those who are willing to listen."

-Longwalker

"In a time of universal deceit, telling the truth is a revolutionary act."

-George Orwell

"An eye for an eye makes the whole world blind."

-Mahatma Gandhi

"The whole aim of practical politics is to keep the populace alarmed and hence, clamorous to be led to safety, by menacing it with endless series of hobgoblins - all of them imaginary."

-Henry Louis Mencken

"The elementary principles of all deception is to attract the enemy's attention to what you wish him to see, and to distract his attention from what you do not wish him to see."

-General Sir Archibald Wavell (Memorandum to the British Chiefs of Staff)

Warning: Wake Up!

What do you do when no one listens
and all the doors are slammed in your face?

It's such a disgrace to have forgotten our history
What a sin it is to be forsaken
When your voice is lost and all you're left with
are your thoughts, feelings of loneliness start to creep
Inside the wounds cut deep

Wish I could have done more for him
but how is one so young supposed to handle
something so tragically wrong?

Now, we are at world war three as I predicted
back in ninety-three it would be

But in their own selfish demise they turn a blind's eye
just as they've done so many times

Don't you see we are at war with ourselves
when we fight against another?

Open your eyes to all the lies being told
and the scams being sold

Insurance, there's no such thing
and illegal taxation of our nation has caused
so much devastation

Come out of denial so we can smile
When are people going to listen
And heed the warnings?

A change is coming and soon we will know
the answers to all the "whys" and soon
the blind will see then everyone will be sorry
they ever doubted me, please, stop killing me!

Freedom

Democracy does not automatically equate to freedom
True freedom lies within, it can lead to true happiness

I value my freedom more than anything in this world
other than my daughter

And no matter what the situation is, no one can take
your freedom away from you as long as your mind
and spirit are free, then you are free!

Emotions

If emotions or stress aren't released
they hide in the body as disease; Dis-Ease!

Do It Yourself

If you want something done
the way you want it done
don't rely on someone else
do it yourself!

Con

They speak the most brilliant
and wonderful words
soulful, sweet and pure

Words that would make anyone
melt away
but it's all just a game they play
to get the things they want

Selfish and cold
Calculating and cruel
Cunning is their way!

Justification

There is no justifying hurting your child!

Abuse

Always remember

Physical abuse scars the body
Mental abuse scars the mind
And emotional abuse scars the soul!

Rights

We all have a right to believe whatever we believe
and I don't feel anyone should impose their beliefs
onto anyone else

Religious people should not impose their beliefs onto
atheists and atheists should not impose their beliefs
onto religious people

Sure, you have a right to preach and keep preaching
but other people have a right not to listen

And we all have a right to know the real truth about this
world not, just, what's been imposed upon us and fed to
us as being true

Reality

My reality is not your reality
and your reality is not my reality

I do not see through your eyes
and you do not see through my eyes

We may be looking at the same quarter
but from opposite sides

But that does not make what each sees
wrong or obsolete

Being A Shorty

There was an article in the Pasadena/San Gabriel Valley Journal (April 15, 2004) written by Thulani Davis that talked about a recent study conducted by Motivational Educational Entertainment (MEE) where teens and young adults ages sixteen to twenty were interviewed about the heightened disrespect and open disdain for Black women. There was one paragraph in the article that stood out to me and made me realize that the issue of disrespect was not just an adolescent one but an adult one as well. The study refers to the teens as "the hip-hop generation" who are most likely children of the first "hip-hop generation" which is my generation. I know just as many men my age who have the same mentality as this younger generation because they were the first to have this "hip-hop" mentality and they have, now, passed this way of thinking on to their children.

This is definitely a cultural issue and not necessarily an age or generational issue nor is it even an economic issue as this article may have suggested. However, as the article points out most of the adolescents getting pregnant and falling victim are the poor. But I grew up in a small city in upper-white middle-class America, yet still fell prey to this altered world.

I have first-hand experience of this attitude towards Black woman from both men and women. As the authors of the study put it, "Black females are valued by no one" and once sucked in there is no escaping the stigma that are placed on you as a Black female.

The study included a glossary of six nouns used to describe these boys/men (or as I like to call them predators): dog, homeboy, playa, lame, sugar, daddy and payload. The study also included a glossary of nouns (at least 15 of them) used to describe the women: block, bender, woo-woo, flip-flop, skewer, hood-rat, ho and trick to name a few; all meaning promiscuous female. But, in addition, there are freak, bitch, gold-digger, hooch mama, runner, flipper, shorty and wifey (the more ambiguous term).

These predators prey on the weak and vulnerable. The article stated, "A partner whom a male turns to purely for sex, dubbed a shorty, is not a person he wants to take out and there is no escape: once a shorty, always a shorty". Marriage is not a priority, and a committed relationship is often disdained, though some males have steadies they call wifey: that's the chick they (claim to) want to be with (married to). However, both a shorty and a wifey are equally disrespected. I don't think people realize how many wifey's and shorty's are out there and most women don't even realize they are one.

This article made me realize that I have been a shorty and a wifey at some point in my life. I didn't even realize I had been sucked into this culture. I have never been a huge fan of hip-hop, although, I do like some hip-hop artists but I have never liked what the women were doing in the videos or how they were being portrayed and I would not call myself promiscuous. However, I have realized that you do not have to be associated with this culture in order to be stigmatized and labeled like the women of this culture. After reading this article, I realized that I had fallen victim to these predators when I was just fifteen years old and from that moment on I was labeled.

At the age of fifteen, I was preyed on by an older boy who knew exactly what he was doing and how naive I was. He saw my weakness and vulnerabilities and used that against me. I did not have enough knowledge about boys but, more important, I did not have enough self-respect. And it is not just about having self-respect but, also, having a good self-image; a love for one's self.

This is where I plead to all parents, if you want to save your teenage daughters from these "predators", I strongly urge you to instill these positive qualities: self-respect, self-love and a good self-image into your daughters while they are young. This will be their *Suit of Armor* when they come face-to-face with one of these predators. If only someone would have armed me when I was young I would not be, at age 33, just realizing that this is how I, once, was viewed.

Young women and girls are being told that they are only worth having sex with but are not worth being respected, that they are not worth saving if the ship were sinking. Young women and girls, especially young Black girls, are not valued as human beings. However, the saddest part to all this is these males can't and won't see that they don't even respect or value themselves. They do not put themselves into the same categories as they put women.

I want to thank Thulani Davis for writing this article. it has shed some light on a dark culture that very few see or want to acknowledge. It helped me realize that I was once a "shorty" and men won't start respecting women until we start respecting ourselves. From the first night you sleep with a guy you devalue yourself. The men take their cue from us and categorize us. They think sex is all we want and take advantage of our vulnerabilities.

I was never given a *Suit of Armor* to protect me from these predators and I fell prey. I, now, understand that in my life I was never viewed as being more than just a "shorty" or a "wifey" (somebody not worth saving and somebody not worth respecting) because my actions did not show that I was somebody worth marrying, saving or respecting.

Written by Dana Toliver

When Morning Comes

Will I wake to find a better day?

When you don't want tomorrow to come
how do you find the strength to face another day?

When morning comes dig deep into your soul
draw strength from your faith for the courage to carry on

When you are desperately hoping for change to come
and for a dream to turn to reality
find inspiration from a song
know that a better day will come along

Find the strength within
and you will find the answers you seek

When you don't want tomorrow to come
and don't have the courage to carry on

Draw strength from your faith
and hope from your soul
and when morning comes
you will have the courage to face another day

Peace

Peace is the look I see
on my daughter's face
while she's sleeping

Peace is when the heart
and mind are as one

Peace is hearing
an angel's voice
over the phone

Peace is nothing more
than someone's soul at ease

Leap Of Faith

Sometimes when you're walking down your path in life you get to a cliff and the only way to get to the other side and continue on your journey is to take a leap of faith

You have to trust that if you fall your spirit will catch you don't let your fears stop you from taking that leap

Duality

We live in a world of duality
where each one of us
the haves verses the have-nots
has the choice and the right
to choose one or the other

Good or Evil
Heaven or Hell
Positive or Negative
Love or Hate
Peace or War
Right or Wrong
Awake or Asleep

But within this right
you also have a right not to choose

Republican or Democrat
Left or Right
Apple or PC
iPone or Android

but know that with every choice there are consequences
good or bad, so the question becomes:

What choice will you make?

And herein lies the dilemma of every Gemini
Who's not just living in duality but are duality
for we are the only sign that is a twin unto themselves

No matter what choice you choose to make
always remember to never give up your God-given right
to choose because within that choice lies your freedom!

Karma

Love is all we need

Karma, in time will fix
what was never meant to be
No longer will we fear
the powers that be
Stand tall, they will fall

What goes around comes around!

Conventional Wisdom

Brainwashed into believing
that what you look at
isn't really what you see

They've taken away our creativity
the degrees we seek remove us
from our right brain to our left

Taught to not see the obvious
to not use our common sense

Some are trained to see
many dots on a page
without any lines connecting them

While others are trained to only see
horses when hoofs beat
and to not look outside of the box

But it's obvious to see
zebra stripes in a field of horses
the lines connecting the dots on a page
and a window on the side of a box

Just open your eyes and realize
that conventional wisdom
isn't all there is to see!

Death, Fear, Destiny, Love, Karma

Don't be afraid of death
because it is in death
where you find true peace

The root cause of this world's problems is fear
and it's this fear that drives people and motivates them
into action whether it be good, bad or indifferent

But everything happens for a reason and has a purpose
we all have our own destiny's, there are no coincidences

There is a power greater than us, greater than the universe
that's in control of everything, a vast amount of energy
and that power is love which connects us and makes
us one

So when you hurt someone else you are in turn hurting
yourself and that energy will come back to you ten-fold
It May take some time but, eventually
it will come back around

Ignorance Is Bliss

Everyone I know and see around me
is living in ignorance and ignorance is bliss
So, many people choose to stay there

Well, I don't have that luxury of living in bliss
No bliss for me

Being diagnosed with a devastating illness
will rudely wake you up
You stop going through life with blinders on

You wake up to the truth of the corruption
and a system that is designed for destruction
to keep you ignorant to the fact that there is
an agenda so evil most people can't fathom
it exists and that it's designed to kill you

But if you choose to stay alive you must
Remove the blinders and step away from
the bliss of ignorance

Faith

I don't have beliefs
I have facts, knowledge
wisdom and faith

Faith within myself!

Mother Earth

(Inspired by Alonzo Richardson)

Mother Earth does not belong to us
we are her children and we belong to her
we live in her domain

Trust in knowing that she cares
cause she is always there
and she will wash away your pain
through the rain

Understand, that mother nature
holds more power than all of humanity
and she can wipe humanity from existence
if we take her in vain

Have respect for Mother Earth
and you will know your own self-worth

Don't allow humanity to bring you down
trust in her power and she will keep you
safe and sound through your darkest hour

Challenge mother nature and you will lose
you can run but she will catch you
you can hide but she will find you

We must humble ourselves
to the power she possesses
but don't lose hope because Mother Earth
knows what she is doing
for she holds the key to fixing humanity

She is the ultimate expression of truth and love
a mother's love that lies inside you, so keep the faith
because she is our saving grace!

Quotes Two

"It's the soul afraid of dying that never learns to live."
-Amanda McBroom

"Timing is everything and love, sometimes, just isn't enough."
-Dana Toliver

"We had the right love at the wrong time."
-Barry Manilow

"Fear is stronger than love."
-Tupac Shakur

"True happiness is like a butterfly, the more you pursue it the more it will elude you but if you are patient and still it will land softly on your shoulders."
-Unknown

"If everyone could just be still – imagine!"
-Dana Toliver

"If you choose to connect things to something negative then it will be negative but if you choose to connect things to something positive then it will be positive."
-Dana Toliver

State Of Living

My body's breaking down
No one's around
who cares enough
to be concerned about
how it is you really feel
or what it is
you may really need

Stripped from a state of living
To a state of just existing
The sadness in your heart
Pounds with every beat

Longing for the good old days
Wanting a connection
Wishing for healing
Hoping someday
things will get better
Yearning to find love again

You reach out, scream out
Cry out for the world to
Hear you, see you, feel you
But all you are left with is
Feeling broken, disconnected
unwanted and unloved

I wake up and realize that
all of humanity
is in this same state
of just existing

Hoping and wishing
all the sacrifices made
will finally pay off

I see the disconnection
the lost and forgotten souls
I feel the heartache and pain
I hear the silent cries
echoing in the night

To humanity I say
Here is my hand
I am reaching out
Here is my heart
I have all the love to give
Here is my sight
I have the vision
to see into the eyes
of one's soul

So although my body
maybe breaking
My spirit can never be broken

My heart is pure
My love is strong
My vision is clear
I care enough to notice you

The lost, the weak
and the forgotten

If I can't live for me
then I shall live for you
I refuse to just exist!

And The Journey Continues

As you cross over to the spirit world or after life
life lessons will be learned

You will have answers to all the questions
you once yearned for

Your spirit leaves its vessel and will continue on the journey
that your physical body could no longer travel

SECTION FOUR

INSANITY

What's This World Coming To?

What's this world coming to?

The president's lying, education's denying
and history's so un-relying
Families are feuding, kids are fighting
and races are disputing

Got to come together to make things better
Guys killing each other, wars against one another
Come together my brothers
and not just for the sake of one color

It's time for a revolution!

What's this world coming to?

Got to cure disease for the sake of the nation
so we can have a celebration
If we don't mend there will be an end
right before our very eyes
time to say our last goodbyes
It's world war three can't we see?
Look in your mind and be kind
are we too blind to find that bind?

What's this world coming to?

What's up? Listen up!
Youngest of three, want to be free, let me be all I can be
People think I'm dumb, that's for bums
Only God is in position to look down on anyone!

Quotes Three

"When the people fear their government, there is tyranny; when government fears the people, there is liberty"
-Thomas Jefferson

"The greatest strength of government lies in the ignorance of the citizens."
-Max Igan

"We are on the verge of a global transformation. All we need is the right major crisis and the nations will accept the New World Order."
-David Rockefeller

"The individual is handicapped by coming face to face with a conspiracy so monstrous he cannot believe it exists."
-J. Edgar Hoover

"Next the statesmen will invent cheap lies, putting the blame upon the nations that (are) attacked, and every man will be glad of those conscience-soothing falsities, and will diligently study them, and refuse to examine any refutations of them; and, thus, he will by and by convince himself that the war is just, and will thank God for the better sleep he enjoys after this process of grotesque self-deception."
-Mark Twain

"They that can give up essential liberty to obtain a little temporary safety deserve neither liberty nor safety."
-Benjamin Franklin

"It may appear that what goes on is happenstance, but the government most surely has planned it."
-Franklin D. Roosevelt

Lost In The Streets

When I lay me down to sleep
I always start to weep and cry inside for those
who are lost in the streets of darkness and despair
Won't somebody care?
that they are lost in a world that has cast them aside
with nowhere to run and nowhere to hide

Each night that passes by they fight to stay alive
It's a struggle they endure with one thing for sure
If we don't mend it will mean the end
of another innocent one who's life has been lost

When I lay me down to sleep
I always start to weep
I weep for those and pray for those
who are lost in the streets

Come To Peace

It's time to save our countries
from those who insist on destroying them

It's time to take back our world
from the psychopaths who are running it

It's time to save ourselves
from those who are killing us

Everything has been infiltrated
from our food, water and air
to our schools, religion and healthcare

They systematically poison us
themselves and the planet

It's us verses them!
and if the us doesn't come together, soon
we will lose and they will win

Enough of the bickering and fighting against one another
Those days are done!
Come together as one so we can stop the murdering of
millions in the name of oil and democracy

Wake up and see the mass corruption of society

I plead to all my fellow citizens around the world
put down your weapons and come to peace!

Quotes Four

"If you wish to understand the universe, think of energy, frequency and vibration."
-Nikola Tesla

"It is no measure of health to be well adjusted to a profoundly sick society."
-J. Krishnamurti

"Mastering others is strength. Mastering yourself is true power."
-Lao Tzu

"The Illuminati will never possess true power, for they care, only, about mastering others but true power lies within."
-Dana Toliver

"It's not a matter of what is true that counts but a matter of what is Perceived to be true."
-Henry Kissinger

"When the power of love overcomes the love of power, the world Will know peace."
-Jimi Hendrix

"If silence is a cancer, then, secrets are the poison."
-Dana Toliver

The World Today

The world today as we know it to be
No one hears you when you speak
You feel like you don't belong
and, at times, wish you were gone

Don't want to sit by and watch the world go by
while people turn a blind's eye
and pretend they don't see
what is happening to reality

No one knows where the road is going to lead
But they watch as you bleed
This is the world we live in today

Forgive Us

I pray for us humans
for we know not what we do
Mother, please forgive us!

Quotes Five

"If the people only understood the rank injustice of our money and banking system, there would be a revolution before morning."
-Andrew Jackson

"True wisdom is knowing how little we actually know."
-Socrates, Greek Philosopher

"He who passively accepts evil is as much involved in it as he who helps perpetrate it."
-Martin Luther King, Jr.

"This world is not a peaceful place. It's a living hell; a nightmare that's never ending."
-Dana Toliver

"Do not believe anything until it has been officially denied."
-Claude Cockburn

"All war propaganda, all the screaming and lies and hatred, comes invariably from people who are not fighting."
-George Orwell

"There is a crisis in the world, it is a crisis of consciousness."
-Jiddu Krishamurti

"Reality is merely an illusion, albeit a very persistent one."
-Albert Einstein

"A person hears only what they understand."
                                    -Johann Von Goethe

"It's not just waking up to the truth, it's about facing it then dealing with it."
                                    -Dana Toliver

The Question

We talk about being successful as being financially secure
But in the process of becoming financially secure
we tend to lose ourselves; so the question becomes this:

Did you find yourself, your spirit, your purpose and your
pot of gold at the end of the rainbow in your quest
for financial security?

Did you come closer to your creator chasing a white piece
of paper with green ink on It?

I think not!

Credit Cards

Credit cards are nothing more than
a sophisticated tracking system
disguised as a convenient way
to spend money you don't really have
purposefully created to keep you in debt -

It's just another word for control!

Money ($)

Money is the root of all evil
It promotes greed and corruption

In this society
you have to have money in order to make money

And that my friends is America!

Euro-Centricity

Not only am I a woman living in a man's world
Not only am I a Black woman living in a white
Euro-centric, world but I am a Black woman
living in a white, Euro-centric, man's world!

Quotes Six

"The dangerous man, to any government, is the man who is able to think things out for himself. Almost inevitably, he comes to the conclusion, that the government he lives under is dishonest, insane and intolerable."

-H.L. Mencken, American writer (1880-1956)

"Cowardice asks the question – is it safe? Expediency asks the question – is it polite? Vanity asks the question – is it popular? But conscience asks the question – is it right? And there comes a time when one must take a position that is neither safe, nor polite, nor popular; but one must take it because it is right."

-Dr. Martin Luther King, Jr.

"The majority of most humans don't want to know the truth because they fear it; most would rather live in denial and stay in their bubbles, too afraid to pop them and know true freedom."

-Dana Toliver

"Get rid of nonsense fault lines of manufactured division and then through unity of response and non-cooperation with our own enslavement they will not be able to do this."

-David Icke

"When you're born into this world, you're given a ticket to the freak show; when you're born into America, you're given a front row seat."

-George Carlin

"As long as, we the people, keep playing their game, we the people, won't win because the game is rigged."
-Dana Toliver

"Strange game, the only way to win is not to play."
-from the movie *WarGames* (1983)

"When I tell the truth, it is not for the sake of convincing those who do not know it, but for the sake of defending those who do."
-William Blake

High Class Pimps

Record companies pimp out singers
Hollywood pimps out actors
The military pimps out soldiers
Banks pimp out customers
Education pimps out teachers
Conventional medicine pimps out health
Churches pimp out preachers
The NBA, NFL and MLB pimp out players
Big Pharma pimps out medicine
Governments pimp out societies
Courts pimp out judges and lawyers
Religion pimps out the people
The UN pimps out nations
And the Illuminati pimps out the world!

Pyramid Scheme

Free me from this insanity we call society
Free me from the chaos of our communities
Free me from the hypocrisy; we don't live in a democracy
Free me from the prison we call a world
where common sense is slacking
and brotherhood is lacking
Free me from this modern day Robin Hood
where the haves steal from the have-nots

People of the world open your eyes and see
what the coming tides will bring
A wave of corruption that will lead to our destruction

Free me from this place where so many are displaced

It's time for a revolution of non-compliance
to free us from this pyramid scheme of deception

Lies

Don't they know we are tired, tired of hearing the same old story?
Don't they know they are wasting their time trying to drop that line?
Don't they understand we don't want to hear it anymore?

Wake up and recognize it's time to stop the lies!

Congress

Why won't they listen to "we the people"?
They sit there with their noses up in the air
pretending not to notice reality
but once in office they develop a superiority complex
and don't like to play by the rules
For them the rules are forever changing
Impeachment isn't for the betterment of "we the people"
    like they claim
It's their only way to seek their fame

For us to believe that our governments truly care is insane
Just look at daddy Bush and Company
and how they lied about the "war on terror"
9/11 was not an error

For us to think that our votes truly count is a farce
just look at the last presidential "election"
that turned out to be a selection

Insanity

You cannot rationalize with an irrational person
You cannot be logical with an illogical person
You cannot reason with an unreasonable person
And if you do you will drive yourself insane!

But who are we to judge who is irrational, illogical or unreasonable?

Quarter Analogy

Even though two people can be looking at the same quarter doesn't mean they will see the same thing on the quarter. If one person is looking at the quarter from one side and the other person is looking at the quarter from the other side, they will come to two different truths about the same quarter. One person will say they see a tail, the other will say they see a head. It does no mean one person is wrong because the other person sees something different.

The quarter in this scenario represents our multidimensional world. Just because we may not see what someone else sees does not mean what they are seeing isn't real or does not exist and it does not mean they are wrong. Two truths, seemingly in opposition to each other, can both be true, simultaneously.

Hollywood Car Analogy

The writers are the wheels
The producers are the engine
The directors are the steering wheel
The actors are the shell

But without the wheels of a car
it can't move forward

Ten Percent

If we only use ten percent of our brain capacity
and we only know ten percent of what lies in the universe
then don't we only know ten percent of the truth?

The other ninety percent is unknown to us
so how, then, can we realistically say that one book
holds all the answers?

And why, then, is it so hard for some people to believe
that there could be more knowledge and truth that has
yet to be discovered?

Quotes Seven

"There is no one true religion. Religion has been created to distract, separate and mislead people; it is a construct. No one was born religious but everyone was born spiritual."
-Dana Toliver

"The way of heaven can be known and experienced through the heart."
-Manly P. Hall

"Sometimes, if you focus too much on the messenger you wind up missing the message."
-Dana Toliver

"It has been said that something as small as the flutter of a butterfly's wing can ultimately cause a typhoon halfway around the world."
-Chaos Theory

"Truth is not always nice or pretty; often times it is downright ugly."
-Dana Toliver

"Knowing others is intelligence. Knowing yourself is true wisdom."
-Lao Tzu

"The power that is used to enslave us is the power we give to the enslavers."

-David Icke

"I'd rather be broke and living in truth then rich living in ignorance."

-Dana Toliver

The Fungus Among Us

I am battered and beaten
My abuser, a monster called Fungus
That lives among us
Hiding in the shadows
Disrupting our lives
In ways you don't realize
Until one day you wake up
To a nightmare of non-living
Barely existing
The more you resist
The more the abuse persists
There's a category five
Raging inside you
You try to run away
But you can not hide
From the beast inside
That's eating you alive

I have been shattered and broken
By a monster called Fungus
That lives among us
It takes hold with its Molds
And won't let go
It poisons your soul
You wake to realize
You're in a fight for your life
Barely existing
You try to resist
But the abuse persists

There's a raging storm inside
You try to run away
But you can not hide
From this beast inside
That's eating you alive

Face The Reality

There's so much I want to say
there's so much that can't be prayed away
There's so much sadness deep within
so much heartache from the sins
Divided we fall, united we stand
against the real enemy of humanity
The only way to manifest our true destiny is to see
the clouded vision of 2020, it's not always perfect
so, can't you see the game
that's being perpetrated against humanity

Please take me back to Two Zero One Nine
when we still had time
It's time to wake up to the reality of
the Hunger Games' society that's being
implemented right before our very
eyes but disguised as a virus to kill us
There's so much I want to say
there's so much that can't be prayed away

There is a cult, so diabolical,
that for most it is hard to fathom
It's so hard to fathom that they cannot see
the real enemy
The two-headed snake has fooled many
into believing they are free
when in reality humanity has been enslaved
for thousands of years
It brings me to tears

Heed my warning or be led to the slaughter house
If you don't know, now is the time to face the reality
that so many are afraid to face
but you cannot hide, you cannot run away
from the darkness that is coming,
this is only just the beginning

It is time for humanity to face its fears,
learn who the real enemy is
rise up and stand up to take this enemy down!

Until the true is eliminated
real change will not happen
until humanity is willing
to go through the darkness
it will not make it to the light!
We must stand up and fight!

Secret Illusion

Secrets of society
The plight of humanity
It's all a game of hide and seek
That's making our future look so bleak

Remove the blindfolds that cover your eyes
Come out of the darkness and into the sun
See the truth about our His-Story
A story made up to cover up the reality of society

It's all an illusion to confuse you
To the truth about humanity
What you see is what you get
Is all a crock of shit

Life is a game and we've all been played
The reasons for the trials and tribulations
Are not what's been taught but they've been bought
By our minds and our thoughts

Been brainwashed into believing this illusion is real
Makes you feel like you want to kill
Can't believe what you see, it's a shame to be
So blinded by the secrets of society

Truth is out there if you seek it
But it's hidden very deep, disguised as evil
With a mask to deceive you

Wake up to the illusion before it's to late
Or the secrets will seal our fate!

Quotes Eight

"I believe that unarmed truth and unconditional love will have the final word in reality."
-Dr. Martin Luther King, Jr

"My country is the world and my religion is to be good."
-Thomas Paine

"None are more hopelessly enslaved than those who falsely believe they are free."
-J. Wolfgang Von G.

"We live in a world full of pyramid schemes where we get official His-Story from, which does not equate to truth."
-Dana Toliver

"Condemnation without investigation is the height of ignorance."
-Albert Einstein

"Even if you are in a minority of one, the truth is still the truth."
-Mahatma Gandhi

"Injustice anywhere is a threat to justice everywhere."
-Dr. Martin Luther King, Jr.

"You can not solve problems with the same level of consciousness that created them."
-Albert Einstein

"There is no path to peace. Peace is the path."
                                      -Mahatma Gandhi

"The men the American people admire most extravagantly are the greatest liars; the men they detest most violently are those who try to tell them the truth."
                                      -H.L. Mencken

Collective Conscience

The gullibility of humanity is like a robot
programmed to obey every command
punched into a machine, banded together as one
we are trapped in a vision of mediocracy
longing to escape the Matrix
I feel the isolation

Until our conscience awakens
To the bitterness in society
To the truth of humanity's lockdowns
We will never see the light
That will keep us safe and sound

The collective conscience is fading
Drowning in quicksand, suffocating
The tree of life is dying, it's time to take a stand
Let go of your fears, dry your tears
to break through the chains dragging humanity down
I feel the pain

Until our conscience awakens
to the bitterness in this world
and the truth that lies outside the Matrix
humanity will never see the light
that lights our path to freedom

Like a volcanic eruption
It is time for the warriors
to rise up against the darkness
and the diabolical madness
that has paralyzed society into conformity
locking our conscience in a prison cell, collectively

Guardian Angels

Guardian angels
here our pleas
we're down on our knees
please, give us our wings
so we can fly to the skies
far above the evil eyes

Please, allow me to be the voice
for the voiceless

A voice of truth
a voice of compassion
a voice of wisdom
a voice of reason

How many of us have to suffer & die?
How many babies have to cry?

Will we ever find grace
in a world full of disgrace
where so many are displaced?

We are crying out to you
our guardian angels
please, here our pleas
we're on our knees
begging for our wings, please
to fly high above those evil eyes
that tear us down
guardian angels
please, help us off the ground

Tired of the chaos and confusion
and the burdens I bear
So I question my very existence
Am I worthy of still being here?
taking up space, sucking up air
Do I dare?

Guardian angels
hear our pleas
we're down on our knees
please, give us our wings
so we can fly to the skies
far above those evil eyes

The Devil

I could have been set for life
Instead, I am paying the price
Every time I reach out, I get shut out
The Devil doesn't like it when you turn it down
I see the evil that permeates through the space
Of the place where one's heart should go
I've had one too many heartaches
One too many heartbreaks
Been knocked down to the ground
But never have I stayed down

I rise like a phoenix out of the ashes
I will rise so high I will touch the skies, above
There, I will be everything the devil stole from me
And was never able to be, here
Musician, artist, producer, writer, singer, dancer, performer
I will meet my Prince, find true love and happiness

I will know peace

I will trust enough to share the melodies of my life
The words are written from my soul
Someday, you'll know my story, truthfully
Of how the devil stole my life and I never sold my soul

Rainbow

Was I crazy for believing
in that pot of gold at the end of the rainbow?

Was I crazy for dreaming
it would be there for me?

It was just a matter of time
before I would find my rainbow

I knew, for me, at the end of my rainbow
in that pot of gold would be serenity

SECTION FIVE

IN MEMORY

Granddaddy

(October 11, 1980)

I know I saved your life that night
That night I saw you with a gun
When you and her were in that fight

You made up your mind that day
Driven to take your life away
I wish you would have stayed

Too young to understand
At the tender age of nine
That everything would not be fine

Left with the guilt of thinking it was my fault
For not telling someone you had the gun
Nearly cost me my life

Had you stayed alive
I know I would have thrived
The love inside never died

Granddaddy, they don't see the man I knew
So gentle, loving and kind
Wish you would have stayed
So your light could shine through
The darkness that was left behind

Man (1998)

To a man I did not know
May you rest in peace
For your work here is done

To his wife
May you find comfort in knowing
He was not alone

And to his friend, Ray
May you find peace hearing his last words

May we all find comfort in knowing
He's in a better place

To everyone, may we all learn
To open our hearts and let love in

I Saw A Man

I saw a man die today
he won't see another day

The once blue sky
has now turned gray
I saw a man die today

I saw a man take his last breath
that led to his death

The once blue sky is now gray
what a sad, sad day for his widowed wife
though he led a good life

So at seventy-three he is now free
to soar to the once blue sky
that has, now, turned gray

Nine

She lived for the day she would one day
see her house and walk through those doors, again

On December 27, 1998 she saw her dream
manifest into reality and thirteen days later
with stars twinkling in the night she gave up her fight

A piece of me died that I know I'll never get back
no matter how hard I try or how much I cry

Though the memories are great
I know, I can't stop fate

She lived long but something, just, went wrong
She was like fine wine, she grew better with time

But she's an angel now
and with stars shining bright to guide the way
she has gone to heaven on this day

January 8, 1999

She will be missed
now, may she rest in peace
knowing her house is once again a home

And let us all know in our hearts
she has gone to a better place

Through The Darkness (Ben)

– December 5, 2000

Through the darkness there stood Ben
Through all the darkness there was pain
There stood Benjamin Lesane
Through the darkness
I reached out my hand to you
But you could not see; you could not see
All the love surrounding you
And, now, you are free
At the tender age of thirty-three
You grew your wings
You've flown into the wind
And now you will never know that I loved you
But I know you have, finally, found your peace
Until we meet again, my friend
Fly free as a butterfly into the wind
I love you Ben!

A Moment In Time (Tim)

– October 5, 2001

Memories of yesterday fill my mind
A moment in time is all I have left of you and I
I took for granted you would always be there
Your spirit was free and your heart was pure
You were truly something special
We shared a moment in time
And in that moment you touched my heart
You touched the moon and in a moment
You were gone too soon

Carrie

(January 6, 2002)

You were always there
with a calm and quiet presence
yet, courageous and resilient
shining upon my face

This is how I knew Carrie to be
but the wind has taken you
and now you are, finally, at peace
leaving your cares behind
and like a feather blowing in the wind
you are free

With the light guiding the way
and the love of family by your side
you flew into the wind
but you will always be a ray of sunlight
shining down on us from the skies above
as we say goodbye

The Day The Sun Fell Down

(Clarence Hill: Our Fallen Hero)

You were a kind, loving and considerate man
with a quiet, gentle presence who always kept a place
in his heart for everyone; always remembering
everyone's special day

As long as you were here the sun smiled down
with rays of light upon us
but clouds grew close and the rain began to fall

January 15, 2003

Now you are free
and in this time of war you have found your peace
With the rain falling down
and clouds growing close we must say goodbye

But never did I imagine living without our fallen hero
who gave his heart and soul fighting for his country
and fighting for his family

It's hard to see a proud strong man fade away
But he will always be the wind beneath our wings
So when the wind blows, don't be afraid
it's just Clarence with a quiet, gentle presence
on this day the sun fell down

There is solace in the memories
and in knowing we will see the sun again, someday!

A Star Is Born (jiji)

– June 6, 2004

God bless the dreamer
who held steadfast to her dreams
with a warm and gentle spirit

Now watch her spirit rise, high
for the light has come and lifted her to the sky
to carry out her dreams to live forever young and free

The light has carried her home where she belongs
back in the arms of her beloved husband and sisters

Now the three are together again
First Nine then Carrie and now our beloved jiji
a wife, mother, grandmother, aunt, sister and friend to all

I know they are all looking down on us from above
protecting us from the storm, comforting us through the
    rain
keeping us safe and warm

So when raindrops begin to fall on your face
look to the sky and you will see her light shining on
and even though you may feel like your heart has left you
remember, another star has just been born
and it's time for that star to shine

She may be out of our arms reach, now
but she will never be out of our hearts!

Misty Blue

(Barbra Faye Gadson)

We all may be a bit misty eyed
because it is hard to say goodbye
to someone who is loved so dearly

You may want to ask why
but she could no longer stay
and on this day March 31, 2014
she flew away

She has gone home, home to the arms
of her beloved mother

So take comfort in knowing in your heart
she has reached a better place

Remember the music of her grace
and that she always kept the faith

For those who knew
she was sweet as morning dew
so it may be hard to smile now
when you are feeling so misty blue

September Rain

(Joyce Clark) – September 10, 2016

Thank you Joyce for blessing
Jayla and I with your presence
You brought joy and light to our world
But on this day September 10, 2016
The September rain came bringing pain
To the family and friends left behind

You grew your wings
And have flown to the skies above
Leaving behind your spirit of love
You are gone but not forgotten

You will be missed as the rain falls upon us
You were a beautiful soul
But we will find comfort in knowing
You are in the arms of the angels, rejoicing

Jazz

(September 5, 2022)

Little wing you came to me
crying out to save you
but I'm so sorry I missed the signs
clearly, I was blind

You were called to fly
our precious one
Heaven needed you more
you were far too beautiful for this
cold cruel world

Our hearts shattered
and we miss you every moment
of every day
but you put up a valiant fight

The hardest thing I've ever had to do
was walk you to the other side
Will this heartache ever subside?

But thank you for coming
to visit me in my dream
I know your soul is free
and you are happy

No more pain you will ever feel
You are in the arms of Heaven's love
beyond all space and time
I'll cherish the memories, bittersweet

You left your mark with your smile
But the sun has set, our hearts are dark
You are the light we need to breathe

Don't want to let you go
But as we muster the strength to say
Goodbye, Little wing, fly high

R.I.P. – The Day They Found PEACE

Alvin Bracewell (Granddaddy):
October 11, 1980

Tupac Shakur:
September 13, 1996

Princess Diana:
August 31, 1997

The man I didn't know:
1998

Lee Lofton:
December 1998

Fannie Mae Gadson (Nine):
January 8, 1999

Ricardo's Mom:
January 1999

Benjamin Lesane:
December 5, 2000

Timothy Rafael:
October 5, 2001

Aunt Carrie:
January 6, 2002

Robert, John (JD) & G-Mom
October 10, 2002

Clarence Hill:
January 15, 2003

Bertha D. Gadson Toliver Hill (jiji):
June 6, 2004

Verbie Bracewell:
January 10, 2008

Aunt Lueron Williams:
April 19, 2009

Michael Jackson:
June 25, 2009

Raleigh Bryant III:
March 18, 2010

Austin Lacy:
June 2011

Michael Jones:
October 20, 2011

Maurice Thomas Morse:
November 4, 2011

Whitney Houston:
February 11, 2012

Rodney King:
June 17, 2012

Barbra Faye Gadson (Misty):
March 31, 2014

Prince Rogers Nelson:
April 21, 2016

Margaret (Momma) Triplett:
June 14, 2016

Joyce Clark:
September 10, 2016

George Michael:
December 25, 2016

Donald Toliver (Dad):
September 1, 2021

Earnest Hardrict:
November 3, 2021

Jazz Amira Hardrict:
September 5, 2022

SECTION SIX

APPRECIATION

Acknowledgements

JAYLA - Boo, Turtle, you are my "Hero"! Thank you for giving me the strength and courage to keep fighting. You are an awesome daughter! "Love you to the moon and back!"

MOM - I appreciate what you have done for Jayla and I and thank you for not leaving me destitute and without a home.

DAWN - Keep your head up, relax and just breathe! Love you, always!

ROZ - You have been a lifesaver! Thank you for being a great sister and for being there for Jayla and I. You are very much appreciated and loved, always!

LANA- Love you, Sis, always!

LENA- Happy to have you as a sister. Love, always!

VERBA & PAPA CHARLES - Thank you for being such great grandparents to Jayla. Your love and support have been very much appreciated.

FRANCIE - You are a ray of sunshine! Thank you for all of your positive words and encouragement throughout the years!

DALE - Thank you for the support you have given to Jayla. You are very much appreciated!

DAD - I hope you found peace, R.I.P.

RICARDO - A cool brother-in-law!

MAIA - I wish you well.

BRAD - You are loved.

DRAY - SMH! But we created a beautiful daughter, thank you.

ROBERT - I hope you find peace and happiness, someday.

GREG – "Thank you for being there when others were not.

REGGIE – "Desperado", "I Wish You Well"

MARIAH CAREY - Thank you for sharing your voice with the world. Don't stop writing those powerful lyrics that have touched so many hearts and whatever you do keep singing! It was nice to have met you.

DAVID ICKE - You are an inspiration, and your courage is unyielding! Thank you for the awesome work you are doing spreading and speaking the truth! www.davidicke.com

SHARON KRAMER - You are a warrior! Thank you for all the work you have done to bring to light the devastating effects of toxic mold exposure from WDB (water damaged buildings). You are a brave and inspirational woman and your tiresome work will not be in vain. www.katysexposure.wordpress.com

A Tribute To Mariah

I hope "Someday" the "Emotions" of my "Dreamlover" won't be a "Fantasy". He'll "Always Be My Baby" so "Honey" be a "Sweetheart" and "Make It Happen". Come "Stay Awhile" so we can "Fly Away", make "Endless Love" and "Forever", "Till The End Of Time", we'll "Melt Away". I'll "Close My Eyes" and make a wish "Underneath The Stars". "Now That I know" "I Am Free", "All I Ever Wanted" is to give "My All" to a "Vision Of Love". "Do You Think Of Me" because I feel like you are "Slipping Away". "There's Got To Be A Way" "Just To Hold You Once Again". I hope "One Sweet Day" my "Hero" will come back with "Open Arms". "When I Saw You" "Outside" on "The Roof" that "Fourth Of July", "Long Ago", I felt "So Blessed" "To Be Around You". I knew I couldn't live "Without You" and I'd "Never Forget You". The "Music Box" was playing, "The Wind" was blowing through my hair and you whispered softly in my ear, it's not "All In Your Mind", "Love Takes Time", "Anytime You Need A Friend" or "You Need Me" "I'll Be There"! Now, "Whenever You Call" and "I've Been Thinking About You" "And You Don't Remember" the memories we've shared, I feel like a "Prisoner" "All Alone In Love. I "Breakdown" and "I Don't Want To Cry" but "I Can't Let Go" because "Babydoll" I know "The Beautiful Ones" are "Sent From Up Above" so "If It's Over" I think to myself "You're So Cold" but "Looking In" my mind I realize you're simply my "Butterfly" "Vanishing" away. However, "I Still Believe", one day, "When You Believe" there will be a you and me. Just don't be another "Heartbreaker" because I don't want to "Crybaby". "After Tonight" will this "Bliss" return or will it fade like rose "Petals" falling to the ground? Will I be another "X-Girlfriend"? In my "Vulnerability" I used to "Thank God, I Found you", that's "How Much" I loved you! Why "Did I do That"? "Take A Look At Me Now Against All Odds" I have found my "Rainbow" and no one "Can Take That Away"!

Just As Fire Needs Oxygen To Survive
Love Needs Freedom To Flourish
-unknown

What All Gemini's Need 2 Do Is Find
Accept, Embrace Then Master Their Twin Self
-Diamond

II

Gemini's live where dreams are reality
and where reality itself is a dream!
-unknown

If You Don't Stand For Something
You Will Fall For Anything
-unknown

ABOUT THE AUTHOR

 Dana Toliver is a former dancer, gymnast, and assistant teacher. She is a single mother on a mission to help others through writing, blogging and social media platforms. She began writing poetry as a way to cope with childhood trauma and has since created this book in hopes to help others realize they are not alone through their life journey. visit these sites to learn more: www.vocal.media/authors/dana-toliver www.moldcanmakeyousick.wordpress.com

Printed in the USA
CPSIA information can be obtained
at www.ICGtesting.com
CBHW031454271124
18025CB00044B/513